LAKE T...

Travel Guide

Unleash the beauty of Lake Tahoe with stunning scenery, hidden gems, breathtaking landscapes, exhilarating outdoor activities, and vibrant nightlife. Begin your journey to unforgettable memories today!

Hatter Wilder

Table Of Contents

Lake Tahoe, USA.

Lake Tahoe, USA.

Chapter One

Introduction to the Book and Lake Tahoe

This chapter serves as the gateway to the *Lake Tahoe Travel Guide*, offering a comprehensive introduction to the book and the stunning destination of Lake Tahoe. The guide is crafted for travelers of all kinds—families, couples, solo adventurers, and nature enthusiasts—who seek to immerse themselves in the natural beauty, rich culture, and myriad activities this iconic location offers.

The following sections will provide essential insights into what makes Lake Tahoe a remarkable destination. Readers will learn about the unique aspects of the lake, its historical significance, and the region's vibrant culture. They will also discover practical information on how to reach Lake Tahoe and what to expect upon arrival, making their journey as smooth as possible.

Overview of the Book

This travel guide aims to be a complete resource for anyone planning to visit Lake Tahoe. It covers a wide range of topics that address the needs and interests of travelers. From local cuisine and outdoor adventures to wellness retreats and family-friendly activities, this guide provides a comprehensive look at everything Lake Tahoe has to offer.

Each chapter is designed to offer insights and tips that enhance the travel experience. Readers will find detailed recommendations for accommodations, dining, and attractions, along with practical tips for a smooth trip. Whether planning a summer getaway or a winter escape, travelers will find valuable information tailored to their interests.

The book is structured to help readers navigate Lake Tahoe's diverse offerings. The chapters flow logically from an introduction to the area through practical advice, ensuring that visitors can easily find the information they need. Ultimately, this guide aims to inspire and equip travelers for an unforgettable experience at Lake Tahoe.

Introduction to Lake Tahoe

Lake Tahoe is a breathtaking alpine lake situated in the Sierra Nevada mountain range of the United States, straddling the border between

California and Nevada. Known for its stunning blue waters and majestic surroundings, Lake Tahoe is the largest freshwater lake in the Sierra Nevada and one of the deepest lakes in North America. The lake's crystal-clear waters are fed by numerous streams and rivers, and it is surrounded by towering mountains, lush forests, and picturesque beaches.

The beauty of Lake Tahoe is not just in its scenery but also in the diverse activities it offers year-round. In the summer, visitors can enjoy hiking, biking, and water sports, while the winter months bring opportunities for skiing, snowboarding, and cozying up by the fireplace in one of the many lodges. The region is home to numerous parks and recreational areas, making it a paradise for outdoor enthusiasts.

Lake Tahoe is also a cultural hub, with various festivals, art events, and music performances throughout the year. The rich history of the region, influenced by Native American heritage and the Gold Rush era, adds depth to the experience of visiting the lake.

A Brief History and Culture of the Region

The history of Lake Tahoe is both fascinating and rich. For thousands of years, the Washoe Tribe inhabited the area, deeply connected to the land and its resources. They referred to the lake as "da-ow," which means "the lake." Their culture, traditions, and knowledge of the land continue to influence the region today.

In the mid-19th century, the discovery of gold in California brought an influx of settlers to the area, leading to significant changes. Towns sprang up around the lake, and the natural beauty began to attract tourists. By the late 19th and early 20th centuries, Lake Tahoe became a popular destination for wealthy vacationers seeking respite from city life.

Today, Lake Tahoe maintains a unique blend of history and modern culture. Visitors can explore historical landmarks, attend cultural festivals, and appreciate local art that reflects the region's heritage. The ongoing efforts to preserve the natural environment and promote sustainable tourism underscore the community's commitment to protecting the beauty that draws people to the area.

Key Reasons to Visit

There are countless reasons to choose Lake Tahoe as a travel destination. First and foremost is the unparalleled natural beauty. The stunning lake, surrounded by snow-capped mountains and dense forests, offers a visual feast for visitors. The area's diverse landscapes make it perfect for a variety of outdoor activities, whether one is interested in hiking, skiing, or simply relaxing by the water.

In addition to its natural attractions, Lake Tahoe provides a wealth of recreational opportunities. Families can enjoy a variety of activities suitable for all ages, while couples can find romantic spots for dining and relaxation. The range of accommodations—from luxury resorts to cozy cabins—ensures everyone can find a perfect place to stay.

Moreover, the region is rich in cultural experiences. Festivals celebrating music, art, and local traditions abound throughout the year, allowing visitors to engage with the local community and immerse themselves in the culture.

Lastly, Lake Tahoe is easily accessible from major cities in California and Nevada, making it a convenient getaway for short and longer vacations.

How to Get to Lake Tahoe

Traveling to Lake Tahoe is straightforward, with several options available depending on where one is coming from. The closest major airport is Reno-Tahoe International Airport, located approximately 60 miles from the lake. From the airport, visitors can rent a car, take a shuttle, or use public transportation to reach their destination.

For those driving, several highways provide access to Lake Tahoe from various directions. Interstate 80 connects to Highway 89 and Highway 50, both leading directly to the lake. The scenic drive offers stunning views and opportunities to stop at various points of interest along the way.

Travelers coming from California will find numerous routes through picturesque landscapes, including the Sierra Nevada mountains. Those from the Nevada side can easily access the lake via U.S. Route 50.

What to Expect When You Arrive

Upon arrival at Lake Tahoe, visitors will immediately notice the breathtaking scenery that surrounds them. The refreshing mountain air and the sight of the sparkling lake will welcome them. Depending on the season, the atmosphere will vary; summer brings vibrant greenery and bustling activity, while winter offers a peaceful, snow-covered landscape.

As travelers settle in, they will find an array of services and amenities designed to make their stay enjoyable. Visitor centers provide maps, brochures, and information about local attractions. Many hotels and resorts offer friendly staff who can assist with planning activities and dining options.

Exploring the area will reveal charming towns, outdoor adventures, and cultural experiences. Whether visitors seek relaxation on the beach, thrilling outdoor sports, or cultural events, Lake Tahoe has something for everyone.

In conclusion, the Lake Tahoe Travel Guide offers a thorough introduction to this remarkable destination. With its beautiful scenery, rich history, and abundant activities, Lake Tahoe is sure to create lasting memories for all who visit. This chapter sets the stage for the adventure ahead, inviting travelers to immerse themselves in all that this stunning region has to offer.

Chapter Two

Local Cuisine

This chapter focuses on the local cuisine of Lake Tahoe, highlighting the unique flavors and dining experiences that the region has to offer. The food culture in Lake Tahoe is diverse and influenced by its stunning natural surroundings, making it a significant aspect of any visit. Travelers can find a variety of dining options, from casual eateries to upscale restaurants, showcasing local ingredients and culinary traditions.

Visitors will discover that Lake Tahoe's cuisine reflects its geography, climate, and cultural influences. The region's restaurants and food vendors often prioritize fresh, seasonal ingredients, creating dishes that not only satisfy the palate but also celebrate the local environment. This chapter will guide readers through traditional dishes, farm-to-table dining experiences, seafood options, local beverages, and food festivals, encouraging them to indulge in the culinary delights of Lake Tahoe.

Traditional Dishes and Local Flavors

When it comes to traditional dishes, Lake Tahoe offers a delightful range of flavors that reflect the region's history and culture. One of the most iconic dishes is Lake Tahoe trout, a local fish known for its delicate flavor and flaky texture. Many restaurants serve it grilled or pan-seared, often accompanied by seasonal vegetables and locally sourced grains.

Another popular dish is the mountain-style pizza, which features fresh ingredients, unique toppings, and a crispy crust. Visitors often rave about the variety of toppings available, from classic pepperoni to creative combinations that highlight local produce.

Burgers also play a prominent role in Lake Tahoe's dining scene. Many establishments pride themselves on serving high-quality beef, often sourced from local ranches. Guests can enjoy a range of burgers, from classic cheeseburgers to gourmet options topped with unique ingredients like avocado, bacon, and artisan cheeses.

Additionally, visitors should try the chili served in many local establishments. This hearty dish reflects the mountain culture and is perfect for warming up after a day of outdoor activities. Often made with beans, tomatoes, and a blend of spices, each chef adds their personal touch, making it a must-try for anyone looking to savor local flavors.

For dessert, huckleberry pie is a beloved choice. Huckleberries, native to the region, offer a sweet-tart flavor that shines in pies and other desserts. Many bakeries in Lake Tahoe feature this treat, providing a delicious way to end a meal.

Farm-to-Table Dining Experiences

Farm-to-table dining has gained popularity in Lake Tahoe, emphasizing the use of fresh, locally sourced ingredients. This movement not only supports local farmers and producers but also ensures that diners enjoy the highest quality meals. Restaurants committed to this practice often change their menus seasonally, reflecting what is available from local farms.

Visitors can find numerous establishments that prioritize farm-to-table dining. These restaurants feature ingredients such as organic vegetables, grass-fed meats, and locally produced cheeses. The chefs take pride in crafting dishes that celebrate the natural flavors of these ingredients, offering an authentic taste of the region.

In addition to traditional dining, some restaurants offer unique experiences where guests can learn about the sourcing of their food. Farm tours or culinary classes may be available, allowing visitors to connect with local producers and understand the importance of sustainable practices. This hands-on approach enriches the dining experience and fosters a deeper appreciation for the food they enjoy.

Best Places to Enjoy Local Seafood

Lake Tahoe's proximity to the Pacific Ocean allows for a variety of fresh seafood options on local menus. The region is known for its incredible freshwater fish, particularly trout and kokanee salmon, which are often featured in local cuisine. However, many restaurants also offer seafood sourced from the ocean, including shrimp, crab, and seasonal catches.

One of the top places to enjoy local seafood is at the lakeside restaurants, where diners can enjoy stunning views along with their meals. Fish tacos made with fresh catch, or a classic clam chowder, are popular choices. These establishments often highlight the day's catch, ensuring that the seafood is fresh and flavorful.

For a more casual dining experience, seafood shacks and food trucks around the lake serve delicious options such as fish and chips and grilled fish sandwiches. These spots provide a laid-back atmosphere where visitors can enjoy a quick bite while taking in the scenery.

Visitors should also look for restaurants that participate in sustainable seafood practices, ensuring that the seafood they serve is harvested in a way that protects ocean ecosystems. This commitment to sustainability enhances the dining experience while promoting responsible fishing practices.

Wineries, Breweries, and Distilleries

Lake Tahoe's beverage scene is just as vibrant as its food culture, featuring a variety of wineries, breweries, and distilleries. The region is home to several wineries that produce high-quality wines, often from grapes grown in the surrounding areas. Visitors can enjoy wine tastings at local wineries, where they can learn about the winemaking process and sample different varieties, including reds, whites, and rosés.

Craft breweries have also made their mark in Lake Tahoe, offering a wide range of beers, from hoppy IPAs to rich stouts. Many breweries feature tasting rooms where visitors can sample a flight of beers, making it easy to find a new favorite. These breweries often host events, including beer festivals and seasonal celebrations, providing an opportunity for guests to immerse themselves in the local beer culture.

In addition to wineries and breweries, Lake Tahoe is home to distilleries that produce artisanal spirits. Local distilleries often craft small-batch vodka, gin, and whiskey, using ingredients sourced from nearby farms. Tours and tastings at these distilleries give visitors insight into the distillation process while allowing them to savor unique spirits that reflect the region's character.

Food Festivals and Culinary Tours

Food festivals and culinary tours are excellent ways to experience Lake Tahoe's vibrant food scene. Throughout the year, various events celebrate local cuisine, bringing together chefs, farmers, and food enthusiasts. These festivals often feature cooking demonstrations, tastings, and live music, creating a festive atmosphere for all attendees.

One popular event is the Lake Tahoe Food and Wine Festival, where visitors can sample dishes from local restaurants and wineries. This festival showcases the best of the region's culinary offerings, allowing attendees to discover new flavors and meet the chefs behind their favorite dishes.

Culinary tours provide another opportunity to enjoy Lake Tahoe's food scene. These guided tours often take visitors to several restaurants, breweries, or markets, allowing them to taste a variety of dishes and drinks. Tour guides share stories about the local food culture, making it an enriching experience for participants.

In summary, Lake Tahoe's local cuisine is a reflection of its natural beauty and cultural richness. With an emphasis on fresh, local ingredients and a commitment to sustainability, dining in the area is a memorable experience. This chapter encourages readers to savor the flavors of Lake Tahoe, highlighting the importance of experiencing local dishes, beverages, and culinary traditions during their visit. Through the diverse dining options, visitors will gain a deeper appreciation for the region and create lasting memories centered around its cuisine.

Chapter Three

Outdoor Adventures

This chapter focuses on the wide array of outdoor adventures available in Lake Tahoe, making it a prime destination for nature lovers and adventure seekers alike. The region's stunning landscapes, including majestic mountains, lush forests, and the pristine lake itself, provide the perfect backdrop for a multitude of outdoor activities. Whether visitors are seeking a leisurely hike, an adrenaline-pumping ski run, or a serene day on the water, Lake Tahoe offers something for everyone.

The appeal of outdoor adventures in Lake Tahoe lies in the variety of experiences available year-round. Each season brings its opportunities, ensuring that outdoor enthusiasts can enjoy the beauty of nature regardless of the time of year. This chapter will delve into some of the most popular outdoor activities, guiding readers through hiking trails, winter sports, water sports, cycling routes, and fishing excursions. The aim is to encourage visitors to immerse themselves in the natural beauty of Lake Tahoe while engaging in activities that cater to their interests and abilities.

Hiking Trails for All Levels

Hiking is one of the most rewarding ways to experience the natural beauty of Lake Tahoe. The area boasts numerous hiking trails suitable for all skill levels, from easy walks to challenging treks. Whether someone is a seasoned hiker or a family with young children, they can find a trail that meets their needs.

For beginners, the Emerald Bay State Park offers easy-to-navigate trails that lead to breathtaking views of Emerald Bay and its iconic islands. The short hike to the viewpoint is particularly popular, providing a stunning perspective of the clear blue waters and surrounding mountains. Families can enjoy a picnic at one of the many scenic spots along the trail.

More experienced hikers can challenge themselves with trails like the Mount Tallac Trail, which rewards those who venture to its summit with panoramic views of Lake Tahoe and the Sierra Nevada mountains. This hike requires some stamina, but the sense of accomplishment upon reaching the top is well worth the effort. The changing landscapes along the trail, from pine forests to rocky outcrops, create a varied and engaging experience.

For those looking for a unique experience, the Tahoe Rim Trail offers a long-distance hiking option. Stretching over 170 miles around the lake, this trail can be hiked in segments. Hikers can witness a range of ecosystems, from alpine meadows to dense forests, while enjoying spectacular views of Lake Tahoe at different elevations. This trail is perfect for those who enjoy multi-day hikes or simply want to take shorter sections at their own pace.

With so many trails to choose from, Lake Tahoe provides countless opportunities for hikers to connect with nature and enjoy the stunning landscapes at their own pace.

Skiing and Snowboarding in Winter

When winter blankets Lake Tahoe in snow, the region transforms into a premier destination for skiing and snowboarding. With numerous ski resorts dotting the landscape, visitors can find a range of slopes that cater to all skill levels, from beginners to advanced skiers.

Resorts like Heavenly Ski Resort offer a vast array of runs, making it a favorite among locals and tourists alike. Skiers and snowboarders can carve their way down the mountain while taking in breathtaking views of the lake below. For those new to skiing, many resorts provide lessons and rentals, ensuring that everyone can enjoy the thrill of gliding down the slopes.

Another great option is Northstar California Resort, known for its family-friendly atmosphere and well-groomed trails. The resort features terrain parks, ideal for those looking to practice their tricks and jumps. The charming village at Northstar also offers dining and shopping options, making it easy to enjoy a full day on the mountain.

In addition to downhill skiing, visitors can also experience cross-country skiing and snowshoeing in the surrounding areas. Trails at locations like Sugar Pine Point State Park provide a peaceful environment for those seeking a more relaxed pace. Snowshoeing allows participants to venture into the backcountry and discover the serene beauty of the snow-covered landscape.

Winter in Lake Tahoe is a wonderland for outdoor enthusiasts, and the opportunities for skiing and snowboarding are among the best in the country.

Water Sports on the Lake

Lake Tahoe is renowned for its crystal-clear waters, making it a hub for a variety of water sports during the warmer months. Visitors can enjoy activities such as kayaking, paddleboarding, jet skiing, and sailing, all while taking in the stunning views of the surrounding mountains.

Kayaking is a popular choice for those looking to explore the lake at a leisurely pace. Many rental shops around the lake offer kayaks and stand-up paddleboards, allowing visitors to glide across the water and discover hidden coves and beaches. The calm waters of the lake are perfect for beginners, while experienced paddlers can venture further out to enjoy more challenging conditions.

For those seeking a bit more excitement, jet skiing and wakeboarding are thrilling options. Rental services provide access to watercraft, making it easy for visitors to hop on and ride the waves. Several companies offer guided tours, providing an opportunity to learn about the lake's history and geography while enjoying the adrenaline rush of high-speed water sports.

Sailing is another fantastic way to experience Lake Tahoe. Charter services are available for those looking to spend a relaxing day on the water. Visitors can enjoy the gentle breeze and stunning scenery as they sail across the lake, making for an unforgettable day. Some charters even offer sunset cruises, providing a romantic setting as the sun sets over the mountains.

With its pristine waters and stunning views, Lake Tahoe is a paradise for water sports enthusiasts, offering a chance to connect with nature while enjoying a range of activities.

Mountain Biking and Cycling Routes

Mountain biking is a popular activity in Lake Tahoe, with an extensive network of trails designed for cyclists of all levels. The combination of stunning scenery and challenging terrain makes this region a favorite among biking enthusiasts.

Trails such as the Flume Trail offer a unique riding experience with breathtaking views of the lake and surrounding mountains. This relatively moderate trail is well-maintained and provides an exhilarating ride along the cliffs overlooking Lake Tahoe. Cyclists can enjoy the thrill of navigating the twists and turns while soaking in the panoramic vistas.

For those seeking a more challenging experience, the Tahoe Rim Trail also accommodates mountain bikers. Certain sections of this long-distance trail are designated for biking, providing riders with diverse landscapes and stunning views. The combination of elevation changes and varied terrain offers a rewarding challenge for experienced cyclists.

In addition to mountain biking, road cycling is popular in the area, especially around the lake. The scenic routes provide breathtaking views and well-paved roads, making it a great option for both casual riders and serious cyclists. Events like the Tour de Tahoe attract cyclists from all over, showcasing the beauty of the region while promoting a healthy lifestyle.

Lake Tahoe's bike shops and rental services ensure that visitors can easily access the equipment they need. Whether someone is a seasoned biker or just starting, the region's trails offer something for everyone.

Fishing and Nature Tours

Fishing is a cherished activity in Lake Tahoe, with its clear waters teeming with various fish species. Anglers can enjoy a peaceful day on the lake, casting their lines in search of the perfect catch. The most common species include trout, kokanee salmon, and mackinaw, making Lake Tahoe a popular spot for both novice and experienced fishermen.

Several charter companies offer guided fishing tours, providing visitors with the knowledge and expertise needed to make the most of their fishing experience. These tours often include all necessary equipment and tackle, making it easy for visitors to enjoy a day on the water without worrying about logistics. Guides share tips and techniques to enhance the fishing experience, ensuring that everyone has the opportunity to reel in a catch.

For those who prefer to observe nature rather than fish, guided nature tours are also available. These tours often include hiking, wildlife viewing, and learning about the local ecosystems. Knowledgeable guides lead visitors through the breathtaking landscapes, sharing stories about the area's flora and fauna. In their natural habitats, guests may spot local wildlife, such as deer, eagles, and even bears.

In summary, Lake Tahoe is a haven for outdoor adventures, offering a wide variety of activities that cater to all interests and skill levels. Whether someone is hiking scenic trails, skiing down snowy slopes, engaging in thrilling water sports, biking through picturesque routes, or enjoying a peaceful day of fishing, the opportunities for adventure are endless. This chapter encourages visitors to immerse themselves in the beauty of Lake Tahoe's outdoors, reminding them of the joy and fulfillment that comes from connecting with nature. By participating in these activities, they can create lasting memories while experiencing the breathtaking landscapes that Lake Tahoe has to offer.

Chapter Four

Historical Exploration

This chapter focuses on the rich history of Lake Tahoe, a region that has played a significant role in various historical events and cultural developments over the centuries. Visitors to Lake Tahoe can immerse themselves in the area's past through its notable landmarks, museums, and cultural institutions. Each site tells a story, allowing individuals to connect with the region's history in a meaningful way.

Understanding the historical context of Lake Tahoe enhances the experience for travelers. From the days of the Native American tribes who first inhabited the area to the impacts of the Gold Rush and the development of tourism, the history of Lake Tahoe is diverse and compelling. This chapter will guide readers through the key historical sites, museums, and the stories that have shaped the culture and identity of Lake Tahoe. It encourages visitors to appreciate the history of this beautiful region while gaining a deeper understanding of its significance.

Notable Landmarks and Sites

Lake Tahoe is home to numerous landmarks that reflect its storied past. One of the most iconic is Emerald Bay State Park, where visitors can find the picturesque Vikingsholm, a historic mansion built in the 1920s. This remarkable structure is designed in the Scandinavian style and showcases intricate stonework and unique architectural features. A tour of Vikingsholm provides insights into the lifestyle of wealthy summer residents during the early 20th century and offers stunning views of the bay.

Another important landmark is the Tallac Historic Site, which includes several restored buildings that date back to the late 19th century. The site features a museum that highlights the area's early settlement and the development of tourism in Lake Tahoe. Visitors can stroll through the old grounds, learning about the lives of the families who helped shape the region's history.

The Lake Tahoe Historical Society operates the Lake Tahoe History Museum in South Lake Tahoe. This small but informative museum showcases artifacts and exhibits that detail the region's history, including photographs, documents, and tools from the past. A visit to this museum offers a valuable overview of Lake Tahoe's evolution over the years.

These landmarks and sites offer a glimpse into the past, allowing visitors to appreciate the architectural and historical significance of Lake Tahoe.

Museums and Cultural Institutions

In addition to notable landmarks, Lake Tahoe boasts a variety of museums and cultural institutions that preserve and share the area's history. The Nevada State Museum in Carson City, just a short drive from the lake, houses an extensive collection of artifacts related to Nevada's history, including the impact of the mining industry in the region. Exhibits highlight the state's transition from a Gold Rush hub to a popular tourist destination, with a specific focus on Lake Tahoe.

Another significant institution is the Lake Tahoe Community College, which hosts art exhibitions, performances, and educational programs that promote local culture and history. Through various events and workshops, the college engages the community and encourages appreciation for the region's heritage.

Visitors can also find art galleries that focus on local artists and historical themes, showcasing the creativity inspired by Lake Tahoe's stunning landscapes. These cultural institutions play an essential role in preserving the history of Lake Tahoe while fostering an appreciation for the arts.

The Role of Lake Tahoe in the Gold Rush

Lake Tahoe's history is intertwined with the California Gold Rush, a transformative event that drew thousands of prospectors to the West in the mid-19th century. Although Lake Tahoe itself did not yield gold, its strategic location made it a vital stop for those traveling to goldfields in California. The area served as a resting point for weary travelers and a source of supplies.

As the Gold Rush progressed, the region experienced increased activity. Settlers established towns and businesses to support the influx of miners and their families. Towns like Truckee and Virginia City, located nearby, thrived during this period, with many people passing through Lake Tahoe on their way to seek their fortunes.

The Gold Rush era also laid the groundwork for future development in Lake Tahoe. As miners and settlers began to appreciate the area's natural beauty, it attracted the attention of early tourism. The region's stunning landscapes and recreational opportunities began to take shape, leading to the establishment of hotels, lodges, and other amenities that cater to visitors.

Understanding the role of Lake Tahoe in the Gold Rush provides insight into how the region evolved from a resting place for gold seekers to a popular tourist destination.

Native American History and Heritage

Long before the arrival of European settlers, Lake Tahoe was home to Native American tribes, including the Washoe people. These indigenous communities have a deep-rooted connection to the land, with a rich cultural heritage that predates modern history.

The Washoe people utilized the region's natural resources for thousands of years, living in harmony with the land and water. They relied on fishing, hunting, and gathering, fostering a profound respect for the environment. Their cultural practices and traditions continue to be celebrated today, highlighting the importance of preserving their history and heritage.

Visitors can learn about Native American history through cultural events, storytelling sessions, and art exhibits that showcase traditional crafts and practices. Understanding the indigenous perspective enhances the overall experience of Lake Tahoe, providing a deeper appreciation for the land's significance to its original inhabitants.

Famous Historical Figures Connected to Lake Tahoe

Several notable figures have been connected to Lake Tahoe throughout its history. One such figure is Mark Twain, the famous American author, who spent time in the region during the Gold Rush. Twain's experiences in Lake Tahoe inspired some of his writings, capturing the spirit of adventure and exploration that characterized the era.

Another significant figure is John C. Frémont, an explorer and politician who played a crucial role in the westward expansion of the United States. Frémont's expeditions included travels through the Lake Tahoe area, contributing to the growing interest in the region.

Additionally, George Whittell Jr., a prominent businessman, and philanthropist, was instrumental in the development of Lake Tahoe as a tourist destination in the early 20th century. His efforts to preserve the natural beauty of the area led to the establishment of several parks and recreational areas, shaping the way visitors experience Lake Tahoe today.

These historical figures each contributed to the legacy of Lake Tahoe, helping to define its identity and significance in American history.

In conclusion, Lake Tahoe is not only a stunning natural wonder but also a region steeped in history. From its notable landmarks and cultural institutions to its role in the Gold Rush and connections to Native American heritage, the stories of Lake Tahoe are as captivating as their landscapes. This chapter invites visitors to appreciate the rich historical context of the area, encouraging them to engage with the past while enjoying the present. By understanding the history of Lake Tahoe, travelers can create a deeper connection to this remarkable destination, ensuring that their visit is both meaningful and memorable.

Chapter Five

Photography Book

This chapter focuses on the stunning photographic opportunities that Lake Tahoe offers to both amateur and professional photographers. With its breathtaking landscapes, vibrant colors, and unique natural features, Lake Tahoe is a dream location for anyone who enjoys photography. Every angle reveals a different aspect of the region's beauty, making it essential for visitors to understand where to go and what to capture.

Photography is not only about capturing images; it is about telling a story and sharing experiences. In Lake Tahoe, photographers have the chance to document the stunning scenery, from the crystal-clear waters of the lake to the majestic mountains that surround it. This chapter will guide readers through the best photography spots, tips for capturing perfect moments, and opportunities to enhance their skills through professional tours. It encourages everyone, whether a seasoned photographer or a casual visitor with a smartphone, to take advantage of the photographic possibilities that Lake Tahoe presents.

Best Photography Spots Around the Lake

Lake Tahoe boasts numerous photography spots that showcase its stunning natural beauty. One of the most popular locations is Emerald Bay, known for its turquoise waters and the iconic Vikingsholm mansion. This area offers numerous vantage points where photographers can capture both the beauty of the bay and the historic architecture of the mansion. Early mornings and late afternoons provide the best lighting, creating a serene atmosphere that enhances the overall appeal of photographs.

Another excellent spot is Sand Harbor, famous for its striking boulders and clear blue water. This area is ideal for capturing the lake's vibrant colors, especially during sunrise and sunset. Photographers often set up near the water's edge to take advantage of the reflections created by the rocks and the changing colors of the sky.

D.L. Bliss State Park offers more picturesque locations, including sweeping views of the lake and lush pine forests. The park has several hiking trails leading to elevated viewpoints, where photographers can capture the expansive landscape. Each trail provides different angles of the lake, making it a versatile spot for varied photography sessions.

Other notable locations include Incline Village and South Lake Tahoe, both of which provide unique backdrops for photography. Visitors can find charming beaches, scenic trails, and stunning views of the Sierra Nevada mountains, all of which add depth and variety to any photography portfolio.

Capturing Sunrise and Sunset at the Lake

Sunrise and sunset are magical times for photography at Lake Tahoe. During these hours, the light transforms the landscape, creating opportunities for breathtaking images. Early mornings at the lake often present a quiet and peaceful setting, with soft light illuminating the surroundings. Photographers can capture the mist rising from the water, the reflections of the sky on the lake, and the first light hitting the mountains.

Locations such as Cave Rock and Lover's Point are particularly well-suited for sunrise photography. The elevated positions provide sweeping views of the lake, making it easy to capture stunning images as the sun rises above the horizon.

Sunsets at Lake Tahoe are equally captivating. The vibrant colors of the sky create a striking contrast against the blue water, offering photographers a chance to capture dramatic and colorful images. The Sand Harbor area is a favored spot for sunset photography, as the rocks in the foreground complement the brilliant hues of the setting sun.

Planning for these moments is key. Photographers should arrive early to secure a good spot and set up their equipment. Understanding the timing of sunrise and sunset throughout the year can help them make the most of these opportunities, ensuring that they capture the stunning beauty of Lake Tahoe in its best light.

Scenic Overlooks and Viewpoints

Lake Tahoe is dotted with numerous scenic overlooks and viewpoints that provide spectacular photography opportunities. One of the most notable is Mount Tallac, which offers panoramic views of the lake from an elevation of over 9,700 feet. The hike to the summit can be challenging, but the breathtaking views at the top make it worthwhile. Photographers can capture sweeping vistas of the lake, surrounding mountains, and forests, making it an ideal location for landscape photography.

Another fantastic viewpoint is Stateline Lookout, which provides a quick and accessible option for visitors. This viewpoint offers stunning views of the lake, especially during clear days when the colors are vibrant. Photographers can take advantage of the easy access to set up their cameras and capture the beauty of Lake Tahoe without extensive hiking.

Sand Point is another great spot, located within D.L. Bliss State Park. The rocky shoreline provides unique foreground elements for photographs, adding depth to images of the lake. Photographers can capture the interaction between the water and the rocks, along with the stunning views of the surrounding area.

The scenic overlooks throughout the region encourage photographers to discover hidden gems and capture the essence of Lake Tahoe's breathtaking beauty. Each viewpoint offers a unique perspective, inviting individuals to get creative with their shots.

Seasonal Photography Opportunities

Each season at Lake Tahoe presents unique photography opportunities. In the spring, the melting snow creates beautiful waterfalls and vibrant wildflowers that dot the landscape. Photographers can capture the contrast between the rushing water and the blooming flowers, showcasing the region's rebirth after winter.

Summer brings lush greenery and clear blue skies. This season is perfect for capturing outdoor activities and vibrant lake scenes. Photographers can document families enjoying the beach, people hiking, or wildlife emerging in the warmer weather. The longer daylight hours also provide ample opportunities to shoot during golden hours, enhancing the quality of photographs.

Autumn in Lake Tahoe is a photographer's paradise, as the foliage transforms into a stunning array of colors. The changing leaves provide a beautiful backdrop for landscapes, and reflections on the lake create striking images. Photographers can visit areas like Taylor Creek to capture the brilliant colors and the serene atmosphere of the season.

Winter offers a completely different landscape, with snow-covered mountains and frozen lakes. Photographers can capture the beauty of winter sports, the serenity of a snowy landscape, or the unique textures created by snow and ice. Locations such as Heavenly Ski Resort and Northstar California Resort become popular spots for winter photography, where the excitement of skiing and snowboarding contrasts with the peacefulness of snow-covered trees.

Each season brings distinct elements to Lake Tahoe, inviting photographers to adapt their techniques and styles to capture the changing landscape.

Professional Photography Tours

For those looking to enhance their photography skills, professional photography tours are available around Lake Tahoe. These guided tours are led by experienced photographers who share their knowledge and techniques with participants. They provide an excellent opportunity to learn about composition, lighting, and editing, all while exploring the stunning surroundings of Lake Tahoe.

Participants on these tours can benefit from the expertise of professionals who know the best spots for photography, the optimal times to shoot, and tips for capturing the essence of the landscape. Tours may include early morning outings to catch the sunrise or evening excursions to witness the sunset, ensuring that participants make the most of their time in the area.

These tours are suitable for photographers of all skill levels, from beginners eager to learn to advanced photographers seeking to refine their craft. They also offer a chance to connect with fellow photography enthusiasts and share experiences, creating a supportive environment for creativity.

Engaging in a professional photography tour allows individuals to deepen their understanding of the art while capturing breathtaking images of Lake Tahoe's beauty.

In conclusion, Lake Tahoe is a paradise for photography, offering countless opportunities to capture its stunning landscapes and unique features. From the best spots around the lake to seasonal photography possibilities and professional tours, this chapter invites visitors to seize the chance to document their experiences. Whether capturing a serene sunrise, a vibrant autumn scene, or the excitement of winter sports, photographers can create lasting memories through their lens. The beauty of Lake Tahoe awaits, ready to be captured in every frame.

Landscape image of Lake Tahoe viewing the blue sky, USA.

Scenic nature view of boats docked over the calm waters of Lake Tahoe from the rocky boulders on shore in summer, USA.

Chapter Six

Wellness and Relaxation

In today's fast-paced world, finding time for wellness and relaxation has become increasingly important. Lake Tahoe offers an idyllic setting for individuals seeking to unwind and rejuvenate their minds and bodies. The natural beauty of the area, combined with its tranquil atmosphere, creates an ideal environment for wellness activities. From top-notch spas to serene retreats, Lake Tahoe has something for everyone looking to escape the stresses of daily life.

This chapter focuses on the various wellness and relaxation options available in Lake Tahoe. Whether visitors are interested in luxurious spa treatments, yoga sessions by the lake, or discovering natural healing sites, the region offers numerous opportunities to recharge. The abundance of natural beauty, combined with wellness-focused services, makes Lake Tahoe a prime destination for those wanting to invest in their well-being. The following sections highlight the best places and experiences for achieving relaxation and wellness in this beautiful region.

Top Spas and Wellness Retreats

Lake Tahoe is home to several high-quality spas and wellness retreats that cater to those seeking relaxation and rejuvenation. These facilities often combine natural elements with luxurious treatments, ensuring that guests feel pampered and refreshed.

One standout destination is the Lake Tahoe Spa Resort, which offers a range of services, including massages, facials, and body treatments. The serene environment enhances the relaxation experience, allowing guests to unwind completely. Treatments often incorporate local ingredients, providing a unique twist on traditional spa therapies.

Another excellent option is the Spa at Heavenly, located within the Heavenly Ski Resort. This spa offers a variety of treatments designed to soothe sore muscles after a day of skiing or hiking. From deep tissue massages to rejuvenating body wraps, visitors can find the perfect service to help them relax. The spa also features stunning views of the mountains, adding to the overall experience.

For those looking for a comprehensive wellness retreat, The Coachman Hotel offers wellness packages that include yoga classes, meditation sessions, and spa treatments. This retreat encourages guests to focus on their physical and mental well-being, providing a holistic approach to relaxation. The peaceful atmosphere and attentive staff create an inviting space for visitors to disconnect from the outside world.

These spas and retreats provide an excellent opportunity for individuals to invest in their health and well-being, making Lake Tahoe a perfect destination for relaxation.

Yoga and Meditation Experiences

Yoga and meditation are essential components of wellness and relaxation, and Lake Tahoe offers numerous opportunities for individuals to practice these activities. Many local studios and retreat centers provide yoga classes in various styles, accommodating all skill levels.

One popular location is Tahoe Yoga and Wellness Center, known for its diverse range of classes, including Hatha, Vinyasa, and restorative yoga. Classes are often held in serene settings, allowing participants to connect with nature while they practice. The experienced instructors guide students through each session, promoting mindfulness and relaxation.

For those seeking a more immersive experience, several wellness retreats in the area offer specialized yoga programs. These retreats often combine yoga with meditation and other wellness activities, providing a holistic approach to relaxation. Attendees can enjoy morning yoga sessions by the lake, followed by meditation practices that encourage inner peace and self-reflection.

The natural environment of Lake Tahoe enhances the yoga and meditation experience. Many classes take place outdoors, allowing participants to breathe in fresh mountain air and soak in the stunning scenery. This connection with nature fosters a sense of calm, helping individuals to leave behind the distractions of everyday life.

By engaging in yoga and meditation experiences, visitors can cultivate mindfulness and achieve a deeper sense of relaxation during their stay in Lake Tahoe.

Hot Springs and Natural Healing Sites

Natural hot springs and healing sites around Lake Tahoe offer unique opportunities for relaxation and rejuvenation. These geothermal wonders have been cherished for centuries for their therapeutic properties and calming effects on the body and mind.

One popular destination is the Grover Hot Springs State Park, located a short drive from Lake Tahoe. The hot springs are known for their mineral-rich waters, which are believed to provide various health benefits. Visitors can soak in the warm pools while surrounded by stunning mountain views, making it a perfect spot for relaxation.

Another option is Sierra Hot Springs, a serene retreat nestled in the mountains. This facility offers natural hot springs with various temperature options, including outdoor pools that allow guests to enjoy the beauty of nature while soaking. The tranquil atmosphere encourages relaxation and healing, providing an ideal escape from daily stress.

In addition to hot springs, Lake Tahoe is home to several natural healing sites that promote wellness. Areas such as Mount Rose are known for their fresh air and scenic hiking trails, providing opportunities for outdoor exercise and connection with nature. Engaging with the natural environment can enhance overall well-being and encourage relaxation.

Visiting these hot springs and natural healing sites allows individuals to benefit from the therapeutic properties of the water and the serene surroundings. It is an excellent way to unwind and rejuvenate during a trip to Lake Tahoe.

Peaceful Lakefront Resorts

For those seeking a tranquil getaway, Lake Tahoe offers several peaceful lakefront resorts. These accommodations provide a perfect setting for relaxation, with stunning views of the water and easy access to outdoor activities.

One such resort is The Ritz-Carlton, Lake Tahoe, which combines luxury with serene surroundings. Guests can enjoy spa treatments, fine dining, and beautiful views of the lake from their rooms. The resort also offers outdoor activities, including hiking and paddleboarding, allowing visitors to immerse themselves in the natural beauty of the area.

Another excellent option is Edgewood Tahoe, located right on the lake's shore. This resort features a tranquil environment, with opportunities for leisurely walks along the lakefront. Guests can relax on their private balconies, enjoying the peaceful atmosphere while taking in the stunning views. The resort also provides various wellness activities, including yoga sessions and spa treatments, making it an ideal choice for relaxation.

Staying at a peaceful lakefront resort allows visitors to unwind and recharge while enjoying the breathtaking beauty of Lake Tahoe. These accommodations provide the perfect backdrop for relaxation and wellness, encouraging guests to take time for themselves.

Wellness and Relaxation Packages

Many resorts and spas around Lake Tahoe offer specialized wellness and relaxation packages designed to promote self-care and rejuvenation. These packages often combine various services, allowing guests to experience multiple aspects of wellness during their stay.

For instance, some resorts offer packages that include accommodations, spa treatments, and yoga classes. This all-inclusive approach makes it easy for guests to focus on relaxation without worrying about the details. Packages may also include healthy meals and access to wellness activities, ensuring a holistic experience.

Visitors can choose from a range of packages tailored to different needs, whether they are looking for a romantic getaway or a solo retreat focused on personal growth. Many resorts also offer seasonal packages that highlight the unique experiences available in each season, such as winter wellness retreats that incorporate skiing and spa treatments.

By taking advantage of these wellness and relaxation packages, visitors can immerse themselves in a comprehensive experience that promotes healing and rejuvenation. Lake Tahoe's offerings encourage individuals to prioritize their well-being, making it a perfect destination for those seeking relaxation and self-care.

In conclusion, Lake Tahoe is a sanctuary for wellness and relaxation, providing numerous opportunities for visitors to unwind and rejuvenate. From top spas and wellness retreats to yoga experiences and natural healing sites, the region caters to all those looking to prioritize their well-being. Whether staying at a peaceful lakefront resort or engaging in a comprehensive wellness package, visitors can leave behind the stresses of daily life and immerse themselves in the serene environment of Lake Tahoe. The beauty and tranquility of the area create an ideal setting for relaxation, making it a must-visit destination for anyone seeking wellness and rejuvenation.

Chapter Seven

Art and Culture

Art and culture play a vital role in enriching the experience of visiting Lake Tahoe. The region's stunning landscapes and diverse communities have inspired a vibrant artistic scene that includes galleries, music festivals, and public art installations. Visitors can immerse themselves in the local culture through various events and venues that showcase the creativity and talent of the area.

This chapter will delve into the artistic expressions found in Lake Tahoe, highlighting the local art galleries and studios, the rhythm of music festivals and cultural events, the overall vibrancy of Tahoe's art scene, the presence of public art and sculptures, and the significant influence that nature has on local artists. Lake Tahoe is not just a place for outdoor adventures; it is also a haven for those who appreciate creativity and cultural engagement.

Local Art Galleries and Studios

Lake Tahoe is home to a variety of art galleries and studios that feature the works of local and regional artists. These venues provide a unique opportunity for visitors to discover and appreciate the talent present in the area. Each gallery has its distinct personality, showcasing different styles and mediums of art.

One prominent gallery is the Valhalla Tahoe, located within the historic Valhalla Estate. This gallery hosts numerous art exhibitions throughout the year, featuring a range of works from paintings to sculptures. The estate itself is a historic landmark, adding an extra layer of cultural significance to the artwork on display. Visitors can enjoy guided tours of the estate while taking in the artistic offerings.

Another notable destination is the Tahoe Art League Gallery, which promotes local artists and their creations. The gallery often hosts community events and art shows, allowing visitors to interact with the artists and gain insight into their creative processes. The welcoming atmosphere encourages a sense of community and appreciation for the arts, making it a must-visit for art enthusiasts.

Studios around the lake also offer workshops and classes for those interested in creating their art. These hands-on experiences allow visitors to connect with the local artistic community while developing their skills. Engaging in a creative process can be a fulfilling way to spend time in Lake Tahoe.

By visiting the local art galleries and studios, individuals can gain a deeper understanding of Lake Tahoe's culture and the talent that flourishes within its communities. These spaces celebrate creativity and provide a platform for artists to share their work with the world.

Music Festivals and Cultural Events

Lake Tahoe hosts a variety of music festivals and cultural events throughout the year, bringing together locals and visitors to celebrate the rich tapestry of art and culture in the region. These events not only showcase music but also highlight the diversity of the community, making them an essential part of the Lake Tahoe experience.

One of the most anticipated events is the Lake Tahoe Music Festival, which features performances from renowned musicians across genres, including rock, jazz, and folk. The festival typically takes place outdoors, allowing attendees to enjoy music against the backdrop of the beautiful lake and mountains. This combination of great music and stunning scenery creates an unforgettable atmosphere for everyone involved.

Another significant event is the Tahoe City Fine Arts and Crafts Festival. This festival showcases the work of local artisans and craftspeople, offering visitors the chance to purchase unique handmade items. Attendees can also participate in workshops and demonstrations, making it a fun and interactive way to engage with the local art scene.

Cultural events such as art walks and gallery openings are also common in Lake Tahoe. These gatherings allow artists to display their work while fostering connections between the community and visitors. Live music, food vendors, and family-friendly activities often accompany these events, creating a festive atmosphere for all.

Participating in music festivals and cultural events provides an opportunity to connect with the community and experience the artistic vibrancy of Lake Tahoe. It allows individuals to enjoy various forms of expression while enjoying the company of others.

Tahoe's Vibrant Art Scene

The art scene in Lake Tahoe is both vibrant and diverse, reflecting the natural beauty and cultural richness of the area. Artists draw inspiration from the breathtaking landscapes and the spirit of the community, leading to a flourishing artistic environment.

Local artists often gather to share their work and collaborate on projects, creating a supportive network that fosters creativity. Art exhibitions are frequently held at various venues, showcasing everything from contemporary art to traditional crafts. This diversity ensures that there is something for everyone, whether they are art enthusiasts or casual visitors.

The Lake Tahoe Arts Council plays a significant role in promoting the arts in the region. The council organizes events, supports local artists, and provides resources for art education. This dedication to fostering creativity helps maintain a thriving art community, encouraging artists to pursue their passions and share their talents.

In addition to galleries and exhibitions, art can be found throughout the region in unexpected places. Local businesses often display artwork by community artists, creating a gallery-like atmosphere in shops and restaurants. This accessibility allows everyone to appreciate and enjoy the local art scene, making it an integral part of the Lake Tahoe experience.

For those seeking to immerse themselves in the vibrant art scene, Lake Tahoe offers numerous opportunities to connect with local artists, appreciate their work, and witness the creativity that flourishes in this stunning environment.

Public Art and Sculptures

Public art and sculptures add a unique dimension to Lake Tahoe's cultural landscape, enhancing the beauty of the area while encouraging community engagement. Many installations are strategically placed throughout the region, inviting visitors to discover art while enjoying the great outdoors.

One notable piece is the Tahoe Blue Sculpture, located in the heart of South Lake Tahoe. This large, vibrant sculpture reflects the area's stunning blue waters and serves as a symbol of the community's commitment to preserving the environment. It draws the attention of both locals and tourists, becoming a popular photo opportunity.

Another example of public art can be found along the Stateline Art Walk, which features a series of sculptures and installations created by local artists. This outdoor gallery allows visitors to appreciate art while strolling along the lake, making it an enjoyable way to experience the area's cultural offerings.

Community art projects also contribute to the public art scene in Lake Tahoe. Initiatives such as murals and collaborative installations foster a sense of pride among residents and create a lasting impact on the visual landscape of the area. These projects often involve local artists and community members, ensuring that the art reflects the unique character of Lake Tahoe.

Public art and sculptures not only beautify the environment but also engage the community and encourage conversation around art and culture. By interacting with these pieces, visitors can gain a deeper understanding of the artistic spirit that defines Lake Tahoe.

The Influence of Nature on Local Artists

Nature plays a significant role in shaping the work of artists in Lake Tahoe. The stunning landscapes, vibrant colors, and ever-changing seasons provide endless inspiration for creative expression. Many artists draw directly from their surroundings, creating pieces that reflect the beauty and spirit of the region.

Painters, photographers, and sculptors often find their muse in the breathtaking scenery of the lake and mountains. The reflection of the sky on the water, the vibrant hues of autumn foliage, and the serenity of a snow-covered landscape all influence the artistic choices made by local creators. This connection to nature is not just a backdrop; it becomes a fundamental part of their work.

In addition to individual inspiration, nature also serves as a central theme in community art projects. Many local artists collaborate on environmental initiatives, using their talents to raise awareness about conservation and sustainability. This dedication to the environment is evident in their work, as they often seek to highlight the natural beauty of Lake Tahoe and the importance of preserving it for future generations.

The relationship between artists and nature in Lake Tahoe creates a rich cultural tapestry that speaks to the heart of the community. By engaging with local artists and their work, visitors can gain a greater appreciation for the influence of the environment on creativity and artistic expression.

In conclusion, Lake Tahoe is a treasure trove of art and culture that enriches the experience of every visitor. From local galleries and music festivals to public art installations and the profound influence of nature on artists, the region offers countless opportunities to engage with creativity. Visitors can take the time to appreciate the artistic talents that thrive in Lake Tahoe, deepening their connection to the community and the stunning landscape that surrounds them. Embracing the art and culture of Lake Tahoe not only enhances a visit but also fosters a greater understanding of the local spirit and creativity that define this remarkable destination.

Chapter Eight

Family-Friendly Activities

Lake Tahoe is a fantastic destination for families looking for a memorable getaway. With its breathtaking scenery and a variety of activities suitable for all ages, it offers something for everyone. Families can enjoy outdoor adventures, educational experiences, and relaxing moments together. The region's natural beauty serves as the perfect backdrop for creating lasting memories while fostering family bonds.

This chapter focuses on family-friendly activities that make Lake Tahoe an ideal place for children and parents alike. It will cover kid-friendly hiking trails, outdoor parks and playgrounds, family-oriented boat tours and excursions, museums and interactive exhibits for kids, and indoor activities for rainy days. Each of these activities offers unique ways for families to engage with each other while discovering the wonders of Lake Tahoe.

Kid-Friendly Hiking Trails

Hiking is a wonderful way for families to connect with nature, and Lake Tahoe boasts numerous kid-friendly hiking trails that are both accessible and enjoyable for children. These trails offer stunning views, gentle slopes, and educational opportunities, making them perfect for young adventurers.

One of the most popular trails is the Eagle Lake Trail. This short and relatively easy hike, just over a mile round trip, leads families to a picturesque alpine lake surrounded by towering granite cliffs. The trail is well-marked and provides plenty of spots to stop, rest, and enjoy the scenery. Along the way, families can observe the diverse flora and fauna, learning about the local ecosystem while enjoying the fresh mountain air.

Another great option is the Mount Tallac Trail, which offers a more moderate hike for families with older children. While the trail is more challenging, the reward is a breathtaking panoramic view of Lake Tahoe from the summit. Families can take breaks at scenic viewpoints, making it an opportunity for everyone to catch their breath and snap some family photos against the stunning backdrop.

For those looking for a more leisurely hike, the Tahoe Rim Trail has several sections that are suitable for families. This expansive trail encircles the lake and offers numerous access points, allowing families to choose shorter segments that fit their skill level and interests.

These kid-friendly hiking trails not only provide a fun way to get outdoors but also encourage physical activity and an appreciation for the natural world. Hiking together helps families bond while discovering the beauty of Lake Tahoe's landscape.

Outdoor Parks and Playgrounds

Lake Tahoe is home to several outdoor parks and playgrounds that offer families a chance to enjoy recreational activities in a safe and fun environment. These parks are perfect for children to run, play, and interact with others while parents relax or join in on the fun.

Commons Beach in Tahoe City is a great family destination, featuring a spacious grassy area for picnics, beach access for swimming, and a playground for younger children. The beach offers stunning views of the lake and surrounding mountains, making it a perfect spot for a family outing. Families can enjoy activities such as beach volleyball, frisbee, or simply relaxing in the sun. During the summer, the park often hosts events and live music, adding to the vibrant atmosphere.

Another fantastic park is Kings Beach State Recreation Area, which provides plenty of space for families to spread out and enjoy a day outdoors. The park features picnic areas, a sandy beach, and a playground, making it an ideal spot for families to enjoy a variety of activities. Families can swim in the lake, play games on the beach, or take strolls along the shoreline.

For those looking for more structured activities, the Tahoe Donner Recreation Center offers a range of amenities, including a playground, tennis courts, and a swimming pool. Families can enjoy various outdoor games and sports, ensuring that everyone stays active and engaged throughout the day.

Outdoor parks and playgrounds in Lake Tahoe provide families with opportunities for play, relaxation, and quality time together. These spaces encourage kids to be active while allowing parents to unwind and enjoy the beautiful surroundings.

Family-Oriented Boat Tours and Excursions

Boat tours and excursions on Lake Tahoe offer families a unique way to experience the stunning beauty of the lake from a different perspective. These outings are enjoyable for all ages, providing a mix of relaxation, education, and adventure on the water.

One popular option is the Tahoe Gal, a family-friendly paddlewheel boat that offers sightseeing cruises around the lake. These tours typically feature knowledgeable guides who share fascinating stories about the lake's history, geology, and wildlife. Families can enjoy the breathtaking views while learning about the area, making it an educational experience for children.

Another exciting option is the Lake Tahoe Water Taxi, which allows families to explore different parts of the lake at their own pace. This service connects various points around the lake, giving families the freedom to visit different beaches and parks while enjoying the scenic boat ride. Families can hop on and off the water taxi, making it a fun way to discover hidden gems along the shoreline.

For those seeking a more hands-on experience, several companies offer family-oriented kayak and paddleboard rentals. These activities allow families to navigate the calm waters of the lake together, fostering teamwork and providing an exhilarating way to explore the area. Families can choose to take guided tours or venture out on their own, depending on their comfort level and experience.

Boat tours and excursions provide families with memorable experiences on Lake Tahoe, allowing them to appreciate the beauty of the lake from a unique vantage point. These activities encourage bonding while offering fun and adventure for everyone.

Museums and Interactive Exhibits for Kids

For families looking to incorporate educational experiences into their trip, Lake Tahoe offers several museums and interactive exhibits that are both fun and informative. These venues provide children with opportunities to learn through hands-on activities and engaging displays.

The Tahoe Maritime Museum in Homewood is a must-visit for families interested in the history of the lake. The museum features exhibits showcasing the region's maritime heritage, including classic wooden boats and artifacts related to boating and fishing. Families can participate in interactive displays that allow children to learn about the importance of the lake's ecosystem and its historical significance.

Another excellent option is the KidZone Museum in Truckee, designed specifically for children aged 0-7. This interactive museum features a variety of exhibits that encourage imaginative play and creativity. Children can engage in hands-on activities such as art projects, construction games, and role-playing. The museum often hosts special events and workshops, providing families with a dynamic and fun environment to learn and play together.

The Lakeside Inn and Casino often feature art exhibits and community events that include family-friendly activities. Families can enjoy art shows, live performances, and workshops that cater to all ages, allowing everyone to participate in the cultural life of the area.

These museums and interactive exhibits offer families an enriching experience, blending education with fun. By visiting these venues, families can create lasting memories while learning about the rich history and culture of Lake Tahoe.

Indoor Activities for Rainy Days

While Lake Tahoe is known for its beautiful outdoor activities, there are plenty of indoor options for families to enjoy, especially on rainy days. These activities provide a chance to have fun and stay entertained while sheltered from the elements.

One popular indoor option is the South Lake Tahoe Ice Arena, which offers public skating sessions for families. Skating is a great way for everyone to have fun, stay active, and learn a new skill. The rink often hosts special events, including ice hockey games and figure skating performances, adding to the excitement of a day indoors.

For those looking for a bit of adventure, Heavenly Mountain Resort features an indoor rock climbing wall that is suitable for all skill levels. Families can challenge themselves to reach new heights while having fun together. The friendly staff provides guidance and support, ensuring a safe and enjoyable experience for everyone.

Additionally, several movie theaters around Lake Tahoe screen family-friendly films, making it a perfect way to relax and unwind.

Families can enjoy a day at the movies, complete with popcorn and snacks, creating a cozy indoor experience.

For a more creative indoor activity, families can visit art studios or craft centers that offer classes and workshops. These venues allow children to express their creativity while learning new techniques, ensuring a fun and productive indoor experience.

Indoor activities provide families with valuable opportunities to bond while staying entertained, regardless of the weather. By embracing the diverse range of indoor options, families can make the most of their time in Lake Tahoe, creating cherished memories together.

In conclusion, Lake Tahoe is a wonderful destination for families, offering a multitude of activities that cater to all ages. From kid-friendly hiking trails and outdoor parks to boat tours, museums, and indoor fun, families can engage with the natural beauty and cultural richness of the area. Each activity provides an opportunity to create lasting memories and strengthen family bonds. Choosing Lake Tahoe for a family getaway ensures that everyone, from the youngest to the oldest, can enjoy their time together while discovering the joys of this stunning location.

Chapter Nine

Hidden Gems and Off-The-Beaten-Path

Lake Tahoe is renowned for its stunning landscapes and popular attractions, but it also harbors a treasure trove of hidden gems and off-the-beaten-path experiences. These lesser-known spots allow visitors to enjoy a more intimate connection with the area's natural beauty, culture, and history. For those willing to venture beyond the usual tourist hotspots, Lake Tahoe offers unique opportunities to discover tranquil locations, local flavors, and fascinating stories.

This chapter focuses on the hidden gems of Lake Tahoe, including less-known hiking trails, quiet beaches and secret spots around the lake, unique restaurants and cafes, small towns near the lake, and lesser-known historical sites. Each subtopic invites readers to uncover a different facet of the Lake Tahoe experience, promising enriching adventures away from the crowds.

Less-Known Hiking Trails

While many visitors flock to popular trails like the Rubicon Trail or Mount Tallac, Lake Tahoe has a wealth of lesser-known hiking trails that offer stunning views and a chance to immerse oneself in nature without the hustle and bustle of more crowded paths.

One hidden gem is the Angora Lakes Trail, located near South Lake Tahoe. This relatively short hike leads families through lush forests to the picturesque Angora Lakes. The first part of the trail is mostly shaded, providing a comfortable trek even on warm days. Once at the lakes, visitors can enjoy swimming, kayaking, or simply relaxing on the shore. The serene environment makes it an ideal spot for a family picnic, away from the noise of more tourist-heavy areas.

Another less-traveled option is the Van Sickle Bi-State Park Trail, which offers a moderate hike with incredible views of the lake and surrounding mountains. Starting from the South Lake Tahoe area, this trail winds through a mix of pine forest and open areas, providing numerous vantage points to appreciate the stunning scenery. The quiet nature of this trail allows hikers to fully engage with the sights and sounds of the forest.

For those seeking a more secluded experience, the Mount Judah Loop Trail presents an opportunity to hike through alpine meadows filled with wildflowers during the summer months. This trail is less frequented, making it a perfect choice for families or individuals looking to escape the crowds and enjoy nature in a peaceful setting.

These hidden hiking trails not only offer beautiful views but also allow visitors to appreciate Lake Tahoe's natural environment at a leisurely pace, making for memorable outdoor experiences.

Quiet Beaches and Secret Spots Around the Lake

Lake Tahoe is famous for its beautiful beaches, but some of the best spots to enjoy the sun and water are tucked away from the busy public areas. These quiet beaches and secret spots provide the perfect escape for families and individuals seeking a tranquil day by the lake.

One such hidden beach is Sand Harbor, located on the eastern shore. While it can be popular, if visitors arrive early in the morning or later in the afternoon, they can find quieter moments to enjoy the stunning turquoise waters and soft sandy shores. Families can relax, swim, or take a scenic stroll along the shoreline.

For a more secluded experience, the Secret Cove is a true hidden gem. Accessible by a short hike from the main road, this small beach offers stunning views and crystal-clear waters, perfect for swimming or picnicking. The serene atmosphere and picturesque surroundings create a perfect setting for families looking to spend quality time together without the distractions of larger beaches.

Another secret spot is the Kings Beach State Recreation Area, which features a more laid-back environment compared to other beaches. Families can enjoy grassy areas for picnics, shady spots for relaxation, and soft sandy shores for playing and swimming. The quieter ambiance here makes it ideal for families with young children who want to enjoy a day at the lake without the crowds.

These quiet beaches and secret spots around Lake Tahoe offer families a chance to unwind and connect with nature in a serene setting. These hidden treasures provide the perfect backdrop for creating lasting memories.

Unique Restaurants and Cafes

Lake Tahoe is home to a variety of unique restaurants and cafes that offer delightful culinary experiences away from the usual dining spots. These hidden gems often reflect the local culture and showcase the region's culinary creativity.

One standout is the Log Cabin Cafe, located in South Lake Tahoe. This charming diner serves hearty breakfast and lunch options, featuring locally sourced ingredients and a cozy atmosphere. The walls are adorned with photographs and memorabilia, giving it a unique character. Families can enjoy classic American dishes while soaking in the welcoming ambiance.

Another gem is Sushi Pier, a hidden spot known for its fresh sushi and Japanese cuisine. Tucked away in a small plaza, this restaurant offers a diverse menu that caters to both sushi lovers and those looking for cooked dishes. The friendly staff and vibrant atmosphere make it a great place for families to enjoy a delicious meal together.

For those craving a unique experience, The Brew House offers craft beers and a menu filled with comfort food. Located near the lake, this casual eatery features an outdoor patio where families can enjoy their meals while taking in the views. The laid-back atmosphere and extensive menu ensure that everyone in the family will find something to enjoy.

Exploring these unique restaurants and cafes allows families to sample local flavors while enjoying a more intimate dining experience. Each meal becomes a part of the adventure, creating cherished memories.

Small Towns Near the Lake

The small towns surrounding Lake Tahoe provide a glimpse into the local culture and a chance to escape the hustle and bustle of the main tourist areas. These charming communities offer quaint shops, local eateries, and friendly atmospheres that make them perfect for family outings.

Truckee, located just north of Lake Tahoe, is a picturesque town with a rich history and vibrant arts scene. Families can stroll through the historic downtown area, browsing unique shops and galleries. The town also hosts various festivals throughout the year, offering families opportunities to engage with the local community and enjoy live music and delicious food.

Stateline, which straddles the border between Nevada and California, is another small town worth visiting. Known for its casinos and entertainment, Stateline also features beautiful views of the lake and outdoor activities. Families can enjoy a day of hiking or biking on the nearby trails, followed by dinner at one of the local restaurants.

Kings Beach, located on the north shore, is a charming town known for its laid-back vibe and beautiful sandy beaches. Families can spend the day swimming or picnicking at the beach, followed by a visit to local shops and cafes. The town often hosts community events, providing a wonderful way for families to experience local culture and meet residents.

These small towns near Lake Tahoe offer families a chance to connect with the local community while enjoying unique experiences. Each visit can uncover new memories and discoveries.

Lesser-Known Historical Sites

Lake Tahoe's rich history is reflected in its lesser-known historical sites, which provide families with an opportunity to learn about the area's past while enjoying time together. These sites are often overlooked but are worth visiting for those interested in the unique stories that shape the region.

One such site is the Hellman-Ehrman Mansion in Sugar Pine Point State Park. This historic estate dates back to the early 1900s and offers guided tours that delve into the history of the mansion and its former owners. Families can stroll through the beautiful grounds and learn about the significance of the property in the context of Lake Tahoe's development.

Another fascinating site is the Tahoe City Historical Society, which operates a small museum dedicated to preserving the history of the area. Families can explore exhibits that showcase the region's past, including artifacts from Native American tribes and early settlers. The friendly staff is often available to share stories and insights, making it a valuable experience for children and adults alike.

The Mark Twain Cultural Center is another hidden historical gem. Located in the quaint town of Genoa, this center offers insights into the life and works of Mark Twain, who famously visited the area. Families can enjoy engaging exhibits, storytelling sessions, and special events that celebrate the literary history of the region.

These lesser-known historical sites offer families the chance to learn and discover together. By visiting these unique locations, families can gain a deeper understanding of Lake Tahoe's rich history, making their trip even more meaningful.

In summary, Lake Tahoe is filled with hidden gems and off-the-beaten-path experiences that provide families with the opportunity to connect with nature, culture, and history. From less-known hiking trails and quiet beaches to unique restaurants, small towns, and historical sites, these treasures offer enriching adventures that go beyond the typical tourist attractions. Families seeking memorable experiences and cherished moments will find that the hidden gems of Lake Tahoe hold the key to a truly unforgettable getaway.

Chapter Ten

Seasonal Exploration

Lake Tahoe is a year-round destination, each season offering its unique charm and opportunities for visitors. Understanding the seasonal variations in weather, activities, and local events can greatly enhance the travel experience. The vibrant atmosphere changes from summer's warmth to winter's chill, with spring blossoms and autumn colors creating distinct landscapes. This chapter focuses on the best times of year to visit Lake Tahoe, seasonal activities, wildlife watching, special events, and festivals, and how weather impacts trip planning. Each of these aspects highlights the rich diversity of experiences that Lake Tahoe has to offer throughout the year.

Best Times of Year to Visit Lake Tahoe

The best times to visit Lake Tahoe depend on personal preferences and desired activities. Each season brings a unique experience, catering to different interests.

Summer, from late June to early September, is ideal for those who enjoy outdoor activities like hiking, biking, and water sports. The weather is generally warm and sunny, making it perfect for families and adventure seekers. Summer is when the area buzzes with life, offering numerous festivals and events that celebrate the region's culture.

Fall, from late September to November, is another wonderful time to visit. The changing leaves create breathtaking views, making it perfect for photographers and nature enthusiasts. The weather remains pleasant, and the summer crowds begin to thin, allowing for a more peaceful experience. Fall is also the time for harvest festivals and wine tastings, adding a flavorful twist to the visit.

Winter, from December to March, attracts ski and snowboard enthusiasts. Lake Tahoe is home to several world-class ski resorts, and the snow-covered landscape is enchanting. Winter activities like snowshoeing and sledding are also popular. The holiday season brings festive decorations and events, making it a magical time for families to visit.

Spring, from March to May, is a time of renewal. As the snow melts, wildflowers bloom, and the landscape transforms. This season offers a quieter experience, with fewer crowds and opportunities for spring skiing and hiking. Spring is perfect for those who enjoy milder weather and the beauty of nature waking up after winter.

By considering these seasonal variations, visitors can plan their trips to make the most of what Lake Tahoe has to offer throughout the year.

Activities by Season

Summer activities abound in Lake Tahoe. Families can enjoy swimming, kayaking, and paddleboarding in the lake's crystal-clear waters. Hiking trails, like the Mount Tallac Trail and Eagle Lake Trail, are perfect for exploring the stunning scenery. The summer months also host various events, such as outdoor concerts and farmer's markets, providing fun experiences for all ages.

In the Fall, hiking remains popular as the weather cools, making trails comfortable for exploration. Scenic drives along the lake allow families to witness the spectacular fall colors. The Lake Tahoe Autumn Food and Wine Festival showcases local flavors and culinary delights, providing a wonderful experience for food lovers.

Winter transforms Lake Tahoe into a snowy paradise. Skiing and snowboarding are at the forefront, with resorts like Heavenly Mountain Resort and Northstar California Resort offering excellent slopes. Families can also enjoy snowshoeing, ice skating, and even sledding in designated areas. The holiday season brings festive markets and events, creating a warm and joyful atmosphere.

As the snow melts in Spring, hiking trails re-open and the blooming flowers provide stunning vistas. This is also a great time for birdwatching, as migratory birds return to the area. Families can enjoy activities like mountain biking and fishing as the weather warms, making it a delightful time to experience the natural beauty of the region.

Each season in Lake Tahoe offers a range of activities to suit different interests, ensuring that there is something for everyone to enjoy year-round.

Seasonal Wildlife Watching

Lake Tahoe's diverse ecosystem provides ample opportunities for wildlife watching throughout the year. Each season offers unique chances to observe local fauna in their natural habitats.

In Summer, visitors may spot black bears foraging for food, especially in the early mornings and late evenings. Birds, such as ospreys and eagles, can also be seen soaring above the lake, looking for fish. The vibrant greenery attracts various animals, making it an ideal time for nature enthusiasts to observe wildlife.

Fall brings migration patterns, with many birds leaving the area for warmer climates. This is an excellent time to see various species preparing for winter. Visitors can also observe deer as they prepare for the colder months, often seen grazing in the meadows. The changing leaves create a picturesque backdrop for wildlife watching.

Winter offers a different experience, as many animals enter hibernation or migrate to warmer areas. However, visitors can spot tracks in the snow, indicating the presence of wildlife such as coyotes and foxes. Birdwatchers can enjoy spotting resident species like jays and chickadees, which are often active despite the cold.

In Spring, as the snow melts, wildlife becomes more active. This is a prime time for observing bears emerging from hibernation and elk and deer returning to lower elevations. The blooming wildflowers attract various insects, providing additional opportunities for wildlife enthusiasts to enjoy the natural world.

By considering the seasonal variations in wildlife activity, visitors can enhance their experience and make the most of their time in Lake Tahoe.

Special Events and Festivals Throughout the Year

Lake Tahoe hosts a variety of special events and festivals throughout the year, showcasing the region's culture, arts, and outdoor activities. These gatherings provide opportunities for visitors to engage with the community and participate in unique experiences.

In Summer, the Lake Tahoe Music Festival features performances from renowned musicians, creating an enjoyable atmosphere for families. The Lake Tahoe Shakespeare Festival offers outdoor performances that bring classic plays to life against the backdrop of the lake. These events create memorable experiences for visitors of all ages.

As Fall arrives, the Lake Tahoe Autumn Food and Wine Festival is a highlight, celebrating local cuisine and wines. Families can enjoy tastings, cooking demonstrations, and live music, making it a delightful experience for food lovers. The South Lake Tahoe Oktoberfest also draws visitors, showcasing Bavarian culture through food, music, and activities for children.

During the Winter months, holiday celebrations abound. The Lake Tahoe Winter Wonderland event features festive decorations, light displays, and seasonal activities, creating a magical atmosphere. Various ski resorts also host competitions and events, offering opportunities for families to enjoy winter sports and entertainment.

In Spring, events like the Tahoe Rim Trail Challenge invite outdoor enthusiasts to participate in hiking and running activities while enjoying the scenic beauty of the area. The Lake Tahoe Spring Wine Festival showcases local wines and cuisine, providing a relaxed atmosphere for families to enjoy together.

These special events and festivals throughout the year enhance the Lake Tahoe experience, allowing visitors to engage with the local culture and create lasting memories.

How Does Weather Impact Your Trip Planning

Weather plays a significant role in trip planning for Lake Tahoe. Understanding the climate and seasonal variations can help visitors prepare for their adventures and ensure they make the most of their time in the area.

In Summer, temperatures can reach the 80s and 90s during the day, making it essential to pack sunscreen, hats, and light clothing. Evening temperatures drop, so bringing layers is advisable. Knowing that summer thunderstorms can occur in the afternoons, visitors should plan outdoor activities accordingly and have backup plans in case of rain.

Fall generally offers mild weather, perfect for outdoor activities. However, temperatures can fluctuate, so visitors should dress in layers. It is essential to check the weather forecast, especially during late September and October when conditions can shift quickly.

Winter brings cold temperatures and snowfall, creating ideal conditions for skiing and snowboarding. Planning trips around snow conditions is crucial, as heavy snowfall can lead to road closures and travel delays. Visitors should pack warm clothing and gear suitable for winter sports, along with safety equipment for driving in snowy conditions.

In Spring, weather can be unpredictable, with fluctuating temperatures and occasional snow. Visitors should be prepared for both warm and cold conditions, and having appropriate clothing for hiking and other outdoor activities is vital. This season also marks the transition from winter sports to hiking, making it an exciting time for those looking to enjoy the best of both worlds.

By understanding how weather impacts trip planning, visitors can ensure a smoother experience and make the most of their time in Lake Tahoe, regardless of the season.

In conclusion, Lake Tahoe offers a wealth of seasonal experiences, each providing unique opportunities for adventure, relaxation, and connection with nature. By considering the best times to visit, participating in seasonal activities, enjoying wildlife watching, attending special events, and understanding the weather's impact on trip planning, families can create unforgettable memories throughout the year. Lake Tahoe truly has something to offer everyone, no matter the season, inviting visitors to experience the beauty and charm of this incredible destination.

Emerald Bay, Lake Tahoe, California, USA.

Snow, Winter, Cold Image of Lake Tahoe, USA.

Chapter Eleven

Best Hotels and Their Locations

Finding the right place to stay is essential for an enjoyable trip to Lake Tahoe. With a variety of accommodations available, travelers can choose options that best fit their needs and preferences. Whether seeking luxury, family-friendly settings, cozy cabins, romantic getaways, or unique boutique stays, Lake Tahoe has something for everyone. This chapter will explore the best hotels in the area, detailing their features, locations, and what makes them stand out. Choosing the right hotel can significantly enhance the overall experience, allowing visitors to fully appreciate all that Lake Tahoe has to offer.

Luxury Hotels with Lake Views

For those seeking an upscale experience, Lake Tahoe offers several luxury hotels with stunning views of the lake. One such option is the **Ritz-Carlton Lake Tahoe**, located in the Northstar California Resort area. This five-star hotel features elegant rooms and suites, many of which come with balconies overlooking the lake. Guests can enjoy a range of amenities, including a spa, fine dining, and direct access to ski slopes in winter.

Another exceptional choice is the **Edgewood Tahoe Resort**, which sits on the shores of the lake. This hotel combines luxury with breathtaking scenery. Guests can enjoy beautifully appointed rooms with large windows providing panoramic views of Lake Tahoe. The on-site restaurant offers gourmet cuisine, while the resort's outdoor activities and spa services ensure a relaxing stay.

The **Hyatt Regency Lake Tahoe Resort, Spa, and Casino** is also a luxurious option, located in Incline Village. This resort offers beautiful lakefront views and a private beach. With spacious rooms, a full-service spa, and a casino, it provides various entertainment options for guests. The combination of luxury and natural beauty makes these hotels ideal for travelers seeking a high-end experience at Lake Tahoe.

Family-Friendly Accommodations

Lake Tahoe is a great destination for families, and several hotels cater specifically to their needs. The **Lake Tahoe Resort Hotel** in South Lake

Tahoe is one of the top choices for families. It offers spacious suites with kitchenettes, making it easy for families to prepare meals. The hotel features an indoor pool and a complimentary breakfast, adding convenience to the stay.

Another excellent option is the **Northstar California Resort**, which provides family-friendly accommodations in a ski-in/ski-out setting. Families can enjoy a variety of activities, from skiing in winter to hiking and biking in summer. The resort also has a range of dining options and kids' programs, ensuring that younger guests have plenty to keep them entertained.

The **Basecamp Tahoe City** is a unique and affordable family option, offering a laid-back atmosphere. It features family rooms and easy access to outdoor adventures. The hotel's fire pits and picnic areas create a welcoming environment for families to relax and bond after a day of exploring.

Choosing family-friendly accommodations can make a significant difference in creating a memorable vacation, providing both comfort and convenience for parents and children alike.

Cozy Cabins and Vacation Rentals

For travelers who prefer a more rustic experience, Lake Tahoe has a variety of cozy cabins and vacation rentals available. These accommodations offer a home-away-from-home atmosphere, perfect for families and groups.

The **Tahoe Cabin Company** specializes in unique cabin rentals that provide the perfect blend of comfort and nature. These cabins often feature amenities like full kitchens, hot tubs, and outdoor decks, allowing families to enjoy their surroundings fully. Many cabins are located near hiking trails and beaches, making it easy to access outdoor activities.

Airbnb and **VRBO** also offer a wide range of vacation rentals throughout the Lake Tahoe area. Visitors can find everything from charming lakeside cottages to large homes perfect for family reunions. Renting a cabin allows families to enjoy quality time together while experiencing the beautiful scenery of Lake Tahoe.

Cozy cabins provide an inviting space to unwind after a day of adventures, making them an excellent choice for those looking to immerse themselves in the area's natural beauty.

Hotels for Couples and Romantic Getaways

Lake Tahoe is a popular destination for couples seeking a romantic getaway. Several hotels cater specifically to those looking for a more intimate and luxurious experience.

The **Lake Tahoe Resort Hotel** is an excellent option, offering a romantic atmosphere with spacious suites and beautiful lake views. Couples can relax by the indoor pool or enjoy a candlelit dinner at the on-site restaurant. The hotel's proximity to outdoor activities, such as skiing or hiking, allows couples to enjoy adventure together.

The **Postmarc Hotel and Spa Suites** in South Lake Tahoe is another romantic option, featuring spa suites with whirlpool tubs and fireplaces. This intimate hotel provides a tranquil setting for couples to unwind after a day of exploring. The on-site spa offers a variety of treatments designed for relaxation, enhancing the romantic atmosphere.

For couples seeking a unique experience, the **Alpen Sierra Lodge** offers a charming mountain setting with easy access to both summer and winter activities. Its cozy ambiance, along with features like outdoor hot tubs, makes it a perfect choice for romantic getaways.

Choosing hotels that prioritize comfort and intimacy can create lasting memories for couples looking to celebrate special occasions or simply spend quality time together.

Unique and Boutique Stays

Lake Tahoe also boasts a selection of unique and boutique accommodations that offer something different from traditional hotels. The **Basecamp Tahoe City** is one such option, featuring a trendy design and a relaxed atmosphere. This boutique hotel offers a mix of comfortable rooms and shared spaces, creating a communal vibe for guests. Its proximity to outdoor activities and local dining options makes it an excellent choice for those wanting to immerse themselves in the local culture.

The **Hotel Azure** is another boutique option that combines modern design with a warm atmosphere. Located in South Lake Tahoe, it features stylish rooms and a beautiful outdoor pool area. The hotel's location provides easy access to the lake and nearby attractions, making it a convenient choice for visitors.

For a truly unique experience, the **Sierra-at-Tahoe Resort** offers cozy lodging with easy access to the slopes. This resort emphasizes outdoor activities and has a relaxed, welcoming vibe. Guests can enjoy the beauty of nature while staying in comfortable accommodations that enhance their experience.

Selecting unique and boutique stays allows visitors to enjoy a more personalized experience while discovering the charm of Lake Tahoe.

In conclusion, Lake Tahoe offers a diverse range of accommodations to suit every type of traveler. From luxury hotels with breathtaking lake views to cozy cabins perfect for families, couples looking for romantic getaways, and unique boutique stays, there is something for everyone. Finding the right place to stay can greatly enhance the travel experience, allowing visitors to fully immerse themselves in the beauty and adventure that Lake Tahoe has to offer. Whether guests prefer the elegance of a luxury resort or the warmth of a cabin, they are sure to create lasting memories during their stay.

Chapter Twelve

Best Hospitals and Their Locations

When traveling to Lake Tahoe, being informed about local healthcare options is essential for ensuring a safe and healthy trip. This chapter provides valuable information about the best hospitals and medical facilities in the area, along with important tips for staying healthy while visiting. Knowing where to seek medical assistance can offer peace of mind for travelers, allowing them to focus on enjoying their time in this beautiful destination.

Understanding the local healthcare system is especially important for visitors who may require medical attention due to unexpected illnesses or injuries. Lake Tahoe offers a variety of hospitals, clinics, and emergency care centers that provide quality medical services. This chapter will guide readers through the top medical facilities in the area, what services they provide, and how travelers can ensure their health and safety during their stay.

Top Hospitals in Lake Tahoe

Lake Tahoe is served by several reputable hospitals that provide comprehensive medical care. The **Barton Memorial Hospital**, located in South Lake Tahoe, is one of the main healthcare facilities in the area. This hospital is equipped with advanced technology and a skilled medical staff. It offers a range of services, including emergency care, inpatient and outpatient surgeries, and specialized treatments. The hospital is known for its commitment to patient-centered care and community health programs.

Another important medical facility is the **Tahoe Forest Hospital**, located in Truckee. This hospital provides a wide array of services, including emergency care, surgical services, and rehabilitation. The hospital is recognized for its high-quality care and is an important resource for both residents and visitors in the Lake Tahoe region. It also offers specialized services such as women's health and orthopedic care, making it a comprehensive healthcare provider.

Both hospitals are equipped to handle various medical situations, ensuring that visitors have access to the necessary care during their stay in Lake Tahoe. Knowing the locations and services of these hospitals can provide travelers with confidence as they enjoy their time in the area.

Clinics and Emergency Care Centers

In addition to hospitals, several clinics, and urgent care centers are available for visitors who may need medical assistance outside of standard hospital hours. **Barton Urgent Care** is one such facility, located conveniently in South Lake Tahoe. This clinic provides prompt medical attention for non-life-threatening conditions, such as minor injuries, and illnesses, and preventative care. It is a great option for travelers seeking quick treatment without the long wait times typically associated with emergency rooms.

The **Tahoe Forest Urgent Care**, situated in Truckee, is another reliable option for urgent medical needs. This clinic offers similar services to Barton Urgent Care, including treatment for injuries, infections, and other acute illnesses. Both urgent care centers operate extended hours, making them accessible for travelers who may need assistance during evenings or weekends.

Having information about local clinics and emergency care centers ensures that visitors know where to go for prompt medical assistance if needed. This knowledge allows travelers to enjoy their vacation with the reassurance that healthcare options are readily available.

Medical Services for Travelers

Travelers to Lake Tahoe can take advantage of various medical services designed specifically for visitors. Many hospitals and clinics offer travel medicine consultations, where healthcare providers can advise on vaccinations and medications needed for specific activities or conditions while in the area.

Additionally, local pharmacies, such as **Rite Aid** and **CVS**, provide essential health products and medications. Many of these pharmacies have trained pharmacists available to answer questions about medications and health concerns. They can also assist travelers in managing any ongoing health issues during their visit.

Some medical facilities also offer telehealth services, allowing travelers to connect with healthcare professionals remotely. This can be particularly useful for those who may need advice but prefer to avoid in-person visits. Access to these medical services can significantly enhance a traveler's experience, providing peace of mind and ensuring they remain healthy during their stay.

Health Insurance and Coverage Information

Understanding health insurance coverage is vital for travelers visiting Lake Tahoe. Before the trip, visitors need to check with their insurance provider to understand what services are covered while traveling. Many insurance plans offer coverage for emergency medical care, but specific details may vary.

Travelers without health insurance may consider purchasing travel insurance that includes medical coverage. This can provide added security in case of unexpected medical emergencies. Travelers must read the policy details carefully to ensure they are adequately covered during their trip.

In case of an emergency, visitors should be prepared to present their insurance information at the hospital or clinic. Hospitals in Lake Tahoe are accustomed to working with various insurance providers, ensuring that patients receive the necessary care without undue stress over payment.

Tips for Staying Healthy During Your Trip

Staying healthy while traveling can enhance the overall experience and prevent potential issues during the trip. Here are some practical tips for visitors to Lake Tahoe:

1. Stay Hydrated: The high altitude of Lake Tahoe can lead to dehydration. Travelers should drink plenty of water, especially if participating in outdoor activities.

2. Sun Protection: The sun can be intense at high elevations. Visitors should apply sunscreen regularly and wear hats and sunglasses to protect against UV rays.

3. Physical Activity: While enjoying outdoor activities, travelers should listen to their bodies and avoid overexertion. Gradually acclimating to the altitude can help prevent altitude sickness.

4. Food Safety: Eating fresh, well-prepared meals can help prevent foodborne illnesses. Travelers should be mindful of where they dine and consider trying local cuisine at reputable restaurants.

5. Emergency Contacts: Visitors should have a list of emergency contacts, including local hospitals, clinics, and pharmacies, readily available. This can make it easier to seek assistance if needed.

By taking these simple precautions, travelers can enjoy a healthy and worry-free trip to Lake Tahoe.

In summary, being informed about local healthcare options and taking proactive steps to stay healthy can greatly enhance a visitor's experience in Lake Tahoe. With access to top hospitals, clinics, and emergency care centers, travelers can have peace of mind knowing that quality medical services are available if needed. Understanding health insurance coverage and following health tips can further ensure a safe and enjoyable trip. Being prepared is the key to making the most of a visit to this stunning destination.

Chapter Thirteen

Best Bars and Restaurants

Dining in Lake Tahoe offers visitors a delightful experience filled with diverse culinary options. From lakefront dining to cozy bars, the area is home to numerous establishments that cater to all tastes and preferences. This chapter highlights the best bars and restaurants in Lake Tahoe, showcasing the unique flavors and ambiance that make each spot special.

Whether travelers are looking for a fine dining experience, a casual place to grab a drink, or a family-friendly restaurant, Lake Tahoe has something for everyone. Exploring the dining scene in this picturesque location can enhance a visitor's experience, allowing them to savor the local cuisine and enjoy the beautiful surroundings. The following sections will detail the best dining options available, providing a comprehensive guide for anyone seeking great food and drinks during their stay.

Best Lakefront Dining Experiences

Dining by the water is a highlight of any visit to Lake Tahoe. The **Edgewood Tahoe Restaurant** offers stunning views of the lake and surrounding mountains. Guests can enjoy a seasonal menu featuring fresh, locally sourced ingredients. The restaurant's elegant setting makes it perfect for both special occasions and casual meals. The atmosphere is complemented by a carefully curated wine list, ensuring that each meal is paired perfectly.

Another fantastic option is **Gar Woods Grill & Pier**, located in Carnelian Bay. This restaurant is famous for its lakeside views and relaxed vibe. With a menu that includes delicious seafood and mouthwatering steaks, Garwood provides a memorable dining experience. Visitors often rave about the signature drink, the "Woodsie," a frozen cocktail that perfectly complements the warm, sunny days by the lake.

For those looking for a more casual dining experience, **The Boathouse on the Pier** offers a laid-back atmosphere with beautiful lake views. It features a menu with fresh seafood and classic American fare, making it a popular choice for families and groups. Dining here allows guests to soak in the stunning scenery while enjoying great food.

Top Bars for Cocktails and Craft Beers

Lake Tahoe's bar scene is vibrant, with numerous spots offering creative cocktails and a wide selection of craft beers. **The Loft** in South Lake Tahoe is a standout destination known for its extensive drink menu and sophisticated atmosphere. Bartenders craft innovative cocktails that showcase local ingredients, providing guests with unique flavors to savor. The cozy yet stylish environment makes it an excellent place for a night out with friends or a relaxed evening after a day of outdoor adventures.

For craft beer enthusiasts, **Lake Tahoe AleWorX** is a must-visit. This brewery offers a rotating selection of house-made beers, including IPAs, stouts, and sours. Guests can enjoy their drinks on the outdoor patio while taking in views of the beautiful surroundings. The laid-back atmosphere and friendly staff make it a welcoming spot for both locals and visitors.

Another popular bar is **Himmel Haus**, a German beer garden that brings a taste of Bavaria to Lake Tahoe. With an impressive selection of German and craft beers, along with traditional Bavarian cuisine, Himmel Haus offers a unique dining and drinking experience. Guests can gather on the outdoor patio, creating a lively and fun atmosphere perfect for socializing.

Romantic Dining for Couples

For couples seeking a romantic dining experience, **Cedar House Sport Hotel** in Truckee is a charming option. This intimate restaurant emphasizes farm-to-table dining, with a menu that changes frequently based on seasonal availability. The cozy ambiance, combined with the stunning mountain views, sets the stage for a memorable evening. Couples can enjoy beautifully plated dishes paired with fine wines, making it an ideal choice for a special night out.

Evans American Gourmet Cafe is another romantic destination that offers a unique dining experience. With its intimate setting and personalized service, it is perfect for couples looking to celebrate an anniversary or simply enjoy a night together. The menu features a fusion of American and international flavors, all prepared with care and attention to detail. Guests often appreciate the restaurant's cozy atmosphere and attentive staff, which contribute to a delightful dining experience.

For those wanting to enjoy a meal with a view, **The 19th Hole** at the Tahoe City Golf Course provides a relaxed dining atmosphere with panoramic views of the course and surrounding landscape. The menu includes a variety of dishes that cater to different tastes, making it a great choice for a romantic dinner followed by a stroll.

Family-Friendly Restaurants with Kids' Menus

Lake Tahoe also boasts numerous family-friendly dining options that cater to both adults and children. **The Red Hut Café**, known for its hearty breakfasts and casual atmosphere, is a favorite among families. With a diverse menu that includes pancakes, omelets, and sandwiches, there is something for everyone. The friendly staff and welcoming environment make it a great spot to start the day before heading out for family activities.

Riva Grill on the Lake is another excellent choice for families. This restaurant offers a kids' menu featuring favorites like chicken tenders and mac and cheese. While parents enjoy fresh seafood and delicious entrees, kids can enjoy their meals in a fun and engaging atmosphere. The outdoor patio provides stunning views of the lake, making it a pleasant spot for family dinners.

Sushi Pier is a unique option for families who want to try something different. With a variety of sushi rolls and Japanese dishes, it appeals to both adventurous eaters and those who prefer more traditional options. The restaurant's relaxed vibe ensures that families can enjoy a casual meal together without feeling rushed.

Local Favorites and Hidden Food Gems

Lake Tahoe is home to many local favorites and hidden gems that are worth seeking out. **Mamasake**, a small restaurant located in Stateline, is well-known for its inventive sushi and warm atmosphere. Locals often recommend it for its fresh ingredients and creative rolls, which keep visitors coming back for more.

Another hidden gem is **The Naked Fish**, located in South Lake Tahoe. This restaurant specializes in sushi and Asian fusion dishes, offering a menu that highlights unique flavors and fresh ingredients. The intimate setting makes it a favorite among locals looking for a cozy dinner spot.

For a true taste of the local culture, **Brewforia** is a must-visit. This spot combines a brewery and a food market, allowing guests to sample a variety of craft beers and gourmet food from local vendors. It's an excellent place to discover new flavors while enjoying the vibrant atmosphere.

In summary, Lake Tahoe's dining scene offers a diverse array of options that cater to every taste and occasion. From lakefront dining experiences to cozy bars and family-friendly restaurants, there is something for everyone. Visitors are encouraged to immerse themselves in the local culinary culture, trying different establishments and sampling various dishes. The dining options available in Lake Tahoe are sure to enhance the overall experience, creating lasting memories for all who visit.

Chapter Fourteen

Islands in Lake Tahoe and Best Sites to Visit

Lake Tahoe is not only known for its stunning blue waters and majestic mountains but also for its picturesque islands. These islands add to the charm of the lake, offering unique experiences and breathtaking scenery. This chapter delves into the islands of Lake Tahoe, highlighting their significance, history, and the best sites to visit.

Each island in Lake Tahoe has its character and history. Visitors are often drawn to the beauty and tranquility they provide. Whether interested in hiking, swimming, or simply enjoying the view, these islands offer something for everyone. In this chapter, readers will learn about the islands' key features, including historical sites, wildlife, and popular recreational spots.

Overview of the Islands in Lake Tahoe

Lake Tahoe is home to several notable islands, each providing a unique experience. The most famous is **Emerald Bay**, which is often referred to as an island due to its scenic bay that appears to be surrounded by water. It features **Fannette Island**, the only island in Lake Tahoe. Fannette Island is a popular destination for visitors looking to hike and explore. With its rocky terrain and lush vegetation, the island showcases the natural beauty of the lake.

Another notable island is **Tahoe Island**, which offers stunning views and a variety of recreational opportunities. Though smaller, it is less crowded than some of the other areas around the lake, providing a peaceful retreat for those seeking solitude in nature. Visitors can enjoy activities like swimming, kayaking, and paddleboarding while soaking in the beauty of their surroundings.

In addition to these, **Baldwin Beach** is nearby, providing access to the water and an excellent spot for beachgoers. The combination of sandy beaches and clear waters makes this area a favorite among families and sun-seekers.

Key Historical Sites on the Islands

The islands in Lake Tahoe are steeped in history, adding depth to their natural beauty. **Fannette Island** is particularly noteworthy for its historical significance. It was once home to a small tea house built by **Sir George Henry Thorne** in the early 20th century. Today, the ruins of the tea house still stand, serving as a reminder of the island's past. Visitors can hike to the top of the island to see the remnants and enjoy panoramic views of Emerald Bay.

Another significant historical site is the **Eagle Lake** area, which is accessible by a short hike from the Eagle Lake Trailhead. The trail leads to Eagle Lake, a serene spot surrounded by granite cliffs. The historical context of the area, combined with its natural beauty, makes it a worthwhile destination for those interested in the history of the Lake Tahoe region.

Additionally, the **Tallac Historic Site** on the south shore of Lake Tahoe provides insight into the region's past. It features several historic buildings, including the **Tallac Hotel** and the **Hyer Family House**, both of which date back to the late 19th century. Visitors can take guided tours to learn more about the area's history and the people who once inhabited it.

Boat Tours and Access to the Islands

Accessing the islands of Lake Tahoe is best done by boat. Several companies offer boat tours that provide visitors with an opportunity to see the islands up close while enjoying the beautiful views of the lake. These tours typically include stops at key locations, allowing guests to disembark and explore.

For those looking to rent a boat, several marinas around Lake Tahoe provide rental services. **South Lake Tahoe Marina** and **Ski Run Boat Company** are popular options for boat rentals, allowing visitors to navigate the waters at their own pace. Kayaking and paddleboarding are also available for those who prefer a more personal experience on the water.

It is advisable to check the weather conditions and rental availability ahead of time, especially during peak tourist seasons. Understanding the schedule and routes of the boat tours can help visitors maximize their time on the islands.

Unique Wildlife and Flora on the Islands

The islands in Lake Tahoe are home to a rich variety of wildlife and flora. Visitors can often see **bald eagles, ospreys**, and other bird species soaring above the trees. The islands also provide a habitat for various mammals, including deer and coyotes. Birdwatchers will appreciate the diverse avian population, making it a great destination for photography and nature observation.

In terms of flora, the islands boast a range of native plants, including **ponderosa pines, Jeffrey pines**, and **manzanita bushes**. The unique combination of soil, water, and sunlight creates a diverse ecosystem that thrives in the region's climate. Hikers can enjoy the changing scenery as they traverse the islands, with wildflowers adding bursts of color during the spring and summer months.

Popular Spots for Picnics and Nature Walks

For those looking to enjoy a leisurely day, the islands of Lake Tahoe offer many spots perfect for picnics and nature walks. **Emerald Bay State Park** is a prime location for picnicking, with several designated areas equipped with tables and grills. Families can set up their meals while enjoying the breathtaking views of the bay and surrounding mountains.

Fannette Island also features picnic spots where visitors can enjoy their meals in a serene environment. The island's scenic trails allow for leisurely walks, providing visitors with opportunities to immerse themselves in nature while observing the stunning landscapes.

Another great picnic area is **Baldwin Beach**, where families can spread out their blankets on the sandy shores while the children play in the shallow waters. The combination of sun, sand, and the beauty of Lake Tahoe creates a perfect backdrop for a day spent outdoors.

In conclusion, the islands of Lake Tahoe offer a unique blend of natural beauty, history, and recreational opportunities. With their rich ecosystems, historical significance, and accessible activities, these islands provide a perfect getaway for anyone looking to experience the charm of Lake Tahoe. Visitors are encouraged to take the time to visit these islands, partake in the activities available, and soak in the stunning scenery that surrounds them. Whether hiking, picnicking, or simply enjoying the views, the islands promise a memorable experience for all.

Chapter Fifteen

Best Time to Visit and Why

Choosing the right time to visit Lake Tahoe can significantly enhance a traveler's experience. The region has distinct seasons, each offering unique opportunities for adventure and relaxation. Understanding these seasonal variations is essential for making the most of a trip. This chapter discusses the best times to visit Lake Tahoe, exploring the high and low seasons, weather patterns, popular events, and budget considerations.

By understanding the climate and activities available in each season, travelers can plan their trips to match their interests and needs. Whether seeking winter sports, summer activities, or a peaceful getaway in the off-season, knowing the best times to visit will help ensure a memorable experience in this beautiful area.

High Season vs. Low Season

The high season in Lake Tahoe typically spans from late June through August and December through March. During these months, the area sees a significant influx of visitors. Summer brings warm weather, ideal for outdoor activities such as hiking, biking, and water sports. The demand for accommodations and activities increases, leading to higher prices. During winter, the high season centers around ski resorts, attracting snow enthusiasts eager to hit the slopes.

Conversely, the low season occurs in early spring (April to mid-June) and late fall (mid-October to November). These months are less crowded, providing a more peaceful atmosphere. While some activities may be limited, visitors can still enjoy stunning scenery and lower accommodation rates. This time can be ideal for those looking to avoid crowds while still experiencing the natural beauty of Lake Tahoe.

Travelers should consider their preferences when deciding when to visit. If they seek a lively atmosphere with numerous activities, visiting during the high season is ideal. However, for those who prefer a quieter experience with opportunities for relaxation, the low season may be the better choice.

Weather Patterns and Climate

Lake Tahoe has a varied climate that changes significantly throughout the year. In summer, temperatures can reach the mid-80s°F (around 29°C) during the day, making it perfect for swimming, hiking, and outdoor festivals. Evenings tend to be cooler, providing a comfortable environment for evening gatherings.

In winter, temperatures drop, with daytime highs averaging in the 30s°F (around 1°C to 5°C), making it ideal for skiing and snowboarding. Snowfall can be heavy during this season, creating excellent conditions for winter sports. The scenery transforms into a winter wonderland, attracting visitors looking for snowy adventures.

Spring and fall serve as transitional seasons. Spring sees a gradual warming trend, with daytime temperatures in the 50s°F to 70s°F (10°C to 25°C), but it can also be rainy. Fall showcases vibrant foliage, with temperatures ranging from the 60s°F to 70s°F (15°C to 25°C) during the day. These seasons may experience unpredictable weather, but they offer beautiful landscapes and a quieter atmosphere.

Understanding these weather patterns allows travelers to plan their activities accordingly. Knowing what to expect from the climate will help ensure visitors pack appropriately and select suitable activities for their stay.

Popular Festivals and Annual Events

Lake Tahoe hosts a variety of festivals and events throughout the year, adding to the vibrant culture of the region. Some notable events include:

- Lake Tahoe Music Festival: Held in July, this festival features a range of musical performances from classical to contemporary, set against the backdrop of the beautiful lake.

- Tahoe City Wine Walk: Occurring in June, this event allows visitors to taste local wines while exploring shops and galleries in Tahoe City.

- SnowGlobe Music Festival: This three-day music festival takes place in December, drawing attendees from all over the region to enjoy live performances and a festive atmosphere.

- Fourth of July Celebrations: The area celebrates Independence Day with fireworks over the lake, parades, and community events that attract many visitors.

Attending these festivals can enhance a visitor's experience, offering opportunities to engage with local culture and community. Planning a trip around these events can provide additional enjoyment and unique memories.

Ideal Times for Skiing and Water Sports

Winter is the perfect time for skiing and snowboarding in Lake Tahoe. The best conditions for these sports usually occur from December to February, when the snow coverage is at its peak. Ski resorts like Heavenly, Northstar, and Squaw Valley attract both beginners and experienced skiers. Special deals and packages are often available during the week, making it an excellent time for those looking to save while enjoying winter sports.

In contrast, summer is the prime time for water sports. From June to August, the lake's water temperatures rise, making it suitable for swimming, kayaking, paddleboarding, and jet skiing. Many marinas around the lake offer rental services, making it easy for visitors to engage in water activities. This season also hosts various boat tours that showcase the lake's beauty, allowing travelers to enjoy a day on the water.

Travelers interested in these activities should consider their preferences when choosing their travel dates. Ski enthusiasts will want to plan their trips during the winter months, while those looking to enjoy water activities should aim for summer.

Budget Considerations Based on Season

Budgeting for a trip to Lake Tahoe can vary significantly based on the season. During the high season, travelers may find that prices for accommodations, dining, and activities are higher due to increased demand. Booking in advance is essential during these peak times to secure the best rates and availability.

In the low season, travelers can often find more affordable options. Many hotels and resorts offer discounts and special deals to attract visitors during quieter months. This period can be ideal for families or those traveling on a budget, as prices for activities and dining may also be lower.

Travelers should research and plan to maximize their budgets. Taking advantage of off-peak pricing and seeking out free or low-cost activities can help create a more economical trip.

In summary, understanding the best times to visit Lake Tahoe involves considering the seasons, weather, events, and budget. Each season offers unique opportunities, making it essential for travelers to align their visit with their interests. Whether seeking winter sports, summer fun, or a peaceful getaway, Lake Tahoe has something for everyone. Careful planning will ensure that visitors enjoy all the region has to offer, creating lasting memories in this beautiful destination.

Chapter Sixteen

Attractions in the City

Lake Tahoe is not just a beautiful natural wonder; it is also a vibrant destination filled with attractions that cater to a wide range of interests. Visitors to the area will find numerous landmarks, entertainment options, cultural institutions, shopping districts, and guided experiences that enrich their stay. This chapter discusses the various attractions available in and around Lake Tahoe, emphasizing the must-see sights, engaging activities, and unique experiences that await travelers.

Understanding what the city has to offer can significantly enhance a visit, ensuring that guests make the most of their time in this stunning region. From historical landmarks to lively nightlife and shopping, the attractions in Lake Tahoe offer something for everyone. Whether someone is looking for adventure, relaxation, or cultural enrichment, Lake Tahoe provides plenty of opportunities to create lasting memories.

Popular Landmarks and Must-See Sights

Lake Tahoe is home to many popular landmarks and must-see sights that showcase its natural beauty and rich history. One of the most iconic landmarks is Emerald Bay State Park, known for its breathtaking views of the lake and the picturesque Emerald Bay itself. Visitors can hike along the scenic trails or enjoy a boat ride to Fannette Island, the only island in Lake Tahoe, where a small stone tea house stands.

Another significant landmark is the Tallac Historic Site, which features preserved homes and buildings from the late 1800s, giving insight into the region's history. Guests can wander through the grounds, explore the visitor center, and learn about the area's early settlers.

Sand Harbor is also a must-visit location, famous for its crystal-clear waters and sandy beaches. This area is perfect for swimming, picnicking, or simply relaxing by the lake. The stunning rock formations and views of the surrounding mountains make it a popular spot for photography and leisure activities.

For those interested in history, the Lake Tahoe Historical Society Museum provides an informative experience. The museum features exhibits about the area's past, including Native American history, the development of the resorts, and the environmental changes over the years.

These landmarks not only offer breathtaking scenery but also tell the story of Lake Tahoe's cultural and historical significance, making them essential stops for any visitor.

Entertainment and Nightlife Options

When the sun sets, Lake Tahoe transforms into a lively hub of entertainment and nightlife. The area boasts a variety of options for those looking to unwind after a day of outdoor activities. The Stateline area is particularly well-known for its casinos, including Harrah's Lake Tahoe and MontBleu Resort Casino. These venues offer gaming, live entertainment, and dining options, ensuring that guests have plenty to choose from.

For those preferring a more relaxed atmosphere, local bars and lounges provide excellent options. The Loft Theatre combines dining with entertainment, featuring live performances and a unique culinary experience. Visitors can enjoy dinner while watching a show, making for a memorable evening out.

In addition, various seasonal events, such as outdoor concerts and festivals, are held throughout the year. The Lake Tahoe SummerFest and the Lake Tahoe Music Festival bring live music to the region, offering both locals and visitors a chance to enjoy performances in stunning outdoor settings.

With such a diverse array of entertainment and nightlife options, Lake Tahoe ensures that guests can find something that suits their mood, whether it's a lively night at the casino or a quiet evening at a cozy bar.

Cultural Institutions and Galleries

Lake Tahoe is not only about its natural beauty; it also boasts a rich cultural scene. Several cultural institutions and galleries showcase local art, history, and heritage. The Tahoe Art Haus & Cinema is a unique venue that combines art and film, featuring local artists' works while screening independent films and documentaries.

Another notable institution is the Lake Tahoe Community College (LTCC), which often hosts art exhibits and performances. The college promotes local artists and provides a platform for cultural exchange through various events, workshops, and classes.

The Valhalla Art, Music & Festival is an annual event held in the historic Valhalla Estate, offering a range of performances, art displays, and workshops. This festival emphasizes the connection between art and the stunning natural environment of Lake Tahoe.

Additionally, the North Tahoe Arts Center in Tahoe City provides opportunities to engage with local artists and view their work. The center hosts exhibitions, workshops, and art classes, making it a hub for the community.

These cultural institutions and galleries enhance the experience of visiting Lake Tahoe, allowing guests to appreciate the region's artistic talent and creative spirit.

Shopping Districts and Markets

Shopping in Lake Tahoe offers a mix of local boutiques, souvenir shops, and markets that reflect the unique character of the area. The Heavenly Village is a popular shopping destination, featuring a variety of stores that sell everything from outdoor gear to local art and crafts. Visitors can find unique gifts, clothing, and home décor that showcase the region's spirit.

Tahoe City has a charming shopping scene, with quaint shops and galleries lining the streets. This area is perfect for leisurely strolling while discovering local artisans' work and specialty items. Visitors can stop by local markets for fresh produce and handmade goods, providing a taste of the area's agricultural offerings.

The Truckee River Farmers Market, held during the summer months, showcases local farmers and artisans. Visitors can purchase fresh fruits, vegetables, and handmade products, making it a great way to support local businesses while enjoying the vibrant community atmosphere.

Shopping in Lake Tahoe is not just about acquiring items; it is also an opportunity to connect with local culture and support artisans. The variety of shops and markets available provides a diverse experience for all types of shoppers.

Guided Tours and Local Experiences

For those seeking a deeper understanding of the Lake Tahoe area, various guided tours and local experiences are available. These tours can range from scenic boat cruises on the lake to guided hikes that highlight the area's natural beauty and wildlife. Knowledgeable guides share insights about the region's history, ecology, and hidden gems, making these experiences enriching and informative.

Lake Tahoe Adventures offers a variety of outdoor activities, including guided kayaking, paddleboarding, and hiking tours. These tours are perfect for visitors looking to learn more about the area while enjoying its stunning landscapes.

For a more relaxed experience, local companies provide wine and food tours, showcasing the culinary delights of the region. Participants can taste local wines and sample dishes made from fresh, local ingredients, gaining an appreciation for the flavors that define Lake Tahoe.

Photography tours are also popular, allowing visitors to capture the breathtaking scenery with the guidance of local photographers. These tours focus on finding the best viewpoints and understanding the techniques for capturing stunning images.

Guided tours and local experiences offer travelers the chance to connect with the Lake Tahoe community while discovering the area's beauty and history. Whether seeking adventure, culinary delights, or artistic inspiration, these offerings enhance any visit to Lake Tahoe.

In conclusion, Lake Tahoe is filled with a variety of attractions that cater to every interest. From historical landmarks and lively nightlife to cultural institutions, shopping districts, and guided tours, the city provides numerous opportunities for visitors to engage with the environment and community. Planning a trip that includes these attractions ensures that travelers will create unforgettable memories in this stunning destination. The vibrant atmosphere and diverse offerings of Lake Tahoe invite everyone to immerse themselves in all that it has to offer.

Chapter Seventeen

Practical Tips for a Smooth Trip

Traveling to Lake Tahoe offers a chance to experience stunning natural beauty and a range of outdoor activities. However, ensuring a smooth trip requires some preparation and knowledge of the area. This chapter provides practical tips that will help visitors navigate health and safety, transportation, local customs, and emergency contacts. By keeping these tips in mind, travelers can enjoy their stay without unnecessary stress and make the most of their time in this picturesque region.

Having a clear understanding of practical matters is essential for any traveler. From knowing how to stay safe while enjoying the outdoors to navigating transportation options, these tips are designed to enhance the experience of visiting Lake Tahoe. Being informed allows travelers to focus on creating wonderful memories, rather than dealing with unexpected issues.

Health and Safety Tips for Travelers

Staying healthy and safe while traveling is crucial, especially in a place like Lake Tahoe, where outdoor activities abound. First and foremost, it is essential to stay hydrated. The high elevation of Lake Tahoe can lead to dehydration more quickly than at sea level. Carrying a reusable water bottle and refilling it throughout the day will help travelers maintain proper hydration.

Travelers should also consider applying sunscreen frequently, even on cloudy days. The sun's rays can be more intense at higher altitudes, making it easy to get sunburned. Using a broad-spectrum sunscreen with a high SPF is recommended to protect the skin.

When hiking or participating in outdoor activities, it is wise to wear appropriate clothing and footwear. Sturdy hiking shoes with good grip are vital for navigating various terrains while layering clothes can help accommodate changing weather conditions. Checking the local weather forecast before heading out can also aid in planning the day's activities.

Additionally, having a first-aid kit on hand is a smart choice. Basic supplies, such as adhesive bandages, antiseptic wipes, and pain relievers, can help manage minor injuries or ailments that might occur during outdoor activities.

Lastly, staying informed about local wildlife is important for safety. While animals are part of the natural beauty, maintaining a safe distance and not feeding them is crucial to ensure both personal safety and the well-being of the animals.

Transportation and Getting Around Lake Tahoe

Getting around Lake Tahoe can be enjoyable and straightforward with the right information. The area is well-connected, with various transportation options to help visitors reach their desired destinations. Whether exploring the lake, accessing ski resorts, or visiting nearby towns, understanding transportation choices will make navigating the region easier.

Car Rentals, Public Transport, and Ride-Sharing

For those who prefer the freedom of their vehicle, car rentals are widely available at nearby airports and within the local area. Renting a car allows visitors to explore Lake Tahoe at their own pace, making it easier to access remote trails, scenic viewpoints, and less crowded beaches.

However, public transportation is also an option for travelers looking to reduce their carbon footprint or save on costs. The Tahoe Transportation District operates buses that connect major areas around Lake Tahoe. These buses provide access to popular locations, ski resorts, and shopping areas, making it a convenient choice for those who prefer not to drive.

Ride-sharing services like Uber and Lyft are available in the region as well. They can be particularly useful for getting to and from nightlife areas or when returning from outings after dark. Using ride-sharing can be a safe and easy way to travel without the hassle of parking.

Travelers should consider their plans and preferences when deciding on transportation methods. Having a car rental can provide flexibility, while public transport and ride-sharing offer convenient alternatives.

Local Customs and Etiquette

Understanding local customs and etiquette can enhance the travel experience and show respect for the community. Lake Tahoe has a laid-back atmosphere, but being aware of certain practices can help visitors fit in more seamlessly.

For example, greeting locals with a friendly smile and a simple "hello" can create a welcoming environment. Tipping is appreciated in restaurants, bars, and for services such as shuttle drivers. A standard tip of 15-20% is customary in dining establishments, while other service providers usually appreciate a small gratuity as well.

Visitors should also be mindful of the environment. Lake Tahoe is known for its stunning natural beauty, and it is vital to keep the area clean. Respecting nature by picking up litter and following "Leave No Trace" principles ensures that the region remains beautiful for future generations.

When enjoying outdoor spaces, it is courteous to yield to hikers going uphill on trails and to keep noise levels down to preserve the serenity of the area. Observing local wildlife from a distance is important for both safety and the animal's well-being.

Being aware of these customs will help travelers have a more enjoyable and respectful experience in Lake Tahoe.

Emergency Contacts and Services

Having a list of emergency contacts and knowing where to seek help can provide peace of mind while traveling. In case of a medical emergency, visitors should dial 911 for immediate assistance. There are several hospitals and urgent care facilities in the Lake Tahoe area, including Barton Memorial Hospital and Tahoe Forest Hospital, which offer comprehensive medical services.

Travelers should familiarize themselves with local emergency numbers, including the non-emergency police line and fire department contacts. Having a plan for emergencies can help alleviate anxiety during a trip.

Additionally, travelers should consider having travel insurance that covers medical emergencies and unexpected cancellations. This insurance can offer financial protection and support in case of unforeseen events.

Lastly, knowing the locations of nearby pharmacies and grocery stores can help obtain necessary supplies, whether it's over-the-counter medications or snacks for a day out.

In conclusion, being informed and prepared can significantly enhance the travel experience in Lake Tahoe. By following health and safety tips, understanding transportation options, respecting local customs, and knowing emergency contacts, travelers can enjoy a smooth and worry-free trip. These practical tips serve as a guide for making the most of their visit to this beautiful destination, ensuring that their journey is filled with memorable experiences and adventures. Travelers are encouraged to embrace the opportunity to visit Lake Tahoe, and with the right preparation, they will find themselves enjoying all the beauty and excitement this region has to offer.

Chapter Eighteen

Resources and Contacts

When planning a trip to Lake Tahoe, having the right resources and contacts can make all the difference. This chapter provides essential information that travelers can utilize before and during their visit. By being well-prepared and informed, travelers can enhance their experience, ensuring a smooth journey filled with memorable moments.

From helpful websites and apps for travel planning to important local emergency numbers, understanding these resources is crucial. With so much to see and do in Lake Tahoe, having access to the right information allows travelers to maximize their enjoyment. This chapter serves as a guide to the best resources available, empowering visitors to make the most of their time in this beautiful destination.

Useful Websites and Apps for Travel Planning

In the digital age, various websites and apps can simplify travel planning. A few key websites can help travelers gather valuable information about Lake Tahoe.

- Visit Lake Tahoe: This official tourism website provides comprehensive details on attractions, activities, accommodations, and events. It serves as a one-stop shop for all things related to Lake Tahoe, helping travelers discover what the area has to offer.

- TripAdvisor: This platform is known for its extensive user reviews on hotels, restaurants, and activities. Travelers can gain insights from fellow visitors, helping them choose the best options for their preferences.

- AllTrails: For those interested in hiking, AllTrails is an invaluable resource. It offers maps, reviews, and information on trails, including difficulty levels and estimated times. This helps hikers select the best paths suited to their skill levels and preferences.

In addition to websites, several apps can enhance travel planning.

- Google Maps: A must-have for navigation, Google Maps provides real-time directions, estimated travel times, and information about local businesses. It is especially useful for finding the quickest routes and discovering points of interest along the way.

- Yelp: This app is perfect for finding nearby restaurants and attractions. Users can read reviews, check ratings, and see photos, making it easier to decide where to eat or what to do next.

By utilizing these websites and apps, travelers can gather essential information and make informed decisions about their Lake Tahoe adventure.

Local Emergency Numbers and Services

Safety should always be a priority while traveling. Knowing local emergency numbers and services can provide peace of mind. In Lake Tahoe, visitors should familiarize themselves with the following key numbers:

- Emergency Services: Dial 911 for immediate assistance in case of emergencies, including medical situations, fires, or crimes.

- Non-Emergency Police Line: For non-urgent police matters, travelers can contact the local police department. Each town around Lake Tahoe has its number, and this can be useful for reporting minor incidents or seeking assistance.

- Medical Services: For non-life-threatening medical issues, travelers can contact urgent care facilities or local hospitals. Having the phone numbers for nearby hospitals like Barton Memorial Hospital or Tahoe Forest Hospital can be very helpful.

- Poison Control: In case of poison exposure or ingestion, travelers can reach out to the National Capital Poison Center at 1-800-222-1222 for guidance.

Being aware of these numbers ensures that travelers are prepared for any situation that may arise during their trip.

Travel Blogs, Vlogs, and Recommended Reading

For a more personal touch, travel blogs and vlogs can provide valuable insights and tips from fellow travelers. Many bloggers and vloggers share their experiences in Lake Tahoe, offering recommendations and practical advice.

- The Tahoe Weekly: This local blog covers events, activities, and insights from the Lake Tahoe area. It offers up-to-date information about seasonal happenings, outdoor activities, and dining options.

- YouTube Channels: Several YouTube channels focus on travel experiences in Lake Tahoe. Watching these videos can give potential visitors a visual sense of the area, highlighting various attractions and activities.

In addition to blogs and vlogs, recommended reading can further enrich the travel experience. Guidebooks specific to Lake Tahoe can provide in-depth information about the region's history, culture, and outdoor activities. These resources can enhance a visitor's understanding and appreciation of the area.

Maps and Navigation Tools

Having access to accurate maps and navigation tools is essential for any traveler. In Lake Tahoe, both physical and digital maps can serve as valuable resources.

- Physical Maps: Local visitor centers often provide free physical maps of the area. These maps can be useful for planning routes, identifying trails, and discovering lesser-known locations.

- Digital Maps: In addition to Google Maps, other navigation apps like Waze can help travelers navigate Lake Tahoe's roads. These apps can provide real-time traffic updates, alternative routes, and estimated travel times.

Using maps effectively can prevent travelers from getting lost and ensure they find their way to all the fantastic sites Lake Tahoe has to offer.

Essential Apps for Your Trip

Having the right apps on a smartphone can greatly enhance the travel experience. A few essential apps that visitors may find helpful include:

- Weather Apps: Knowing the weather conditions can help travelers plan their activities effectively. Apps like Weather.com or AccuWeather provide up-to-date forecasts, which can be particularly useful in a region where weather can change rapidly.

- Ski and Snowboard Apps: For winter sports enthusiasts, apps like Ski Tracks and OnTheSnow provide valuable information about snow conditions, trail maps, and lift statuses.

- Local Dining Apps: Besides Yelp, apps like OpenTable can assist in making reservations at popular restaurants in Lake Tahoe. This ensures visitors can enjoy meals without long waits.

By downloading these apps, travelers can keep all the necessary information at their fingertips, making their visit more enjoyable and organized.

In summary, having access to reliable resources and contacts can significantly enhance the travel experience in Lake Tahoe. From utilizing useful websites and apps for travel planning to knowing local emergency numbers and services, visitors are encouraged to equip themselves with this information. By doing so, travelers can enjoy a more informed and enriching experience. With the right preparation, Lake Tahoe can become not just a destination, but a memorable adventure waiting to unfold.

Chapter Nineteen

Entry and Visa Requirements

Understanding entry and visa requirements is a crucial step for anyone planning a visit to Lake Tahoe. This chapter provides detailed information for international travelers, helping them navigate the necessary procedures for a smooth arrival. With a wide range of visitors coming from different countries, it is essential to be informed about the specific regulations that apply.

Knowing entry regulations, local currency details, and language tips can significantly enhance a traveler's experience. Additionally, having a clear budget in mind and understanding what to pack can lead to a more enjoyable and stress-free trip. This chapter aims to provide travelers with the knowledge they need to prepare for their visit to Lake Tahoe effectively.

Entry Regulations for International Travelers

International travelers planning to visit Lake Tahoe must adhere to specific entry regulations. These regulations are essential to ensure a smooth and legal entry into the United States.

1. Visa Requirements: Depending on their nationality, travelers may need a visa to enter the United States. Some countries are part of the Visa Waiver Program (VWP), allowing their citizens to visit the U.S. for up to 90 days without a visa. Travelers from these countries must obtain an Electronic System for Travel Authorization (ESTA) before their trip. Others will need to apply for a tourist visa (B-2) at a U.S. embassy or consulate. Travelers must check their country's requirements well in advance of their trip.

2. Passport Validity: Most travelers must have a passport valid for at least six months beyond their intended stay. This is a standard requirement that applies to many countries. Therefore, it is advisable to check passport validity to avoid any last-minute issues.

3. Customs Regulations: Upon arrival, travelers should be aware of customs regulations concerning what they can bring into the U.S. Certain items, such as fresh fruits, vegetables, and some animal products, are

restricted or prohibited. Visitors should declare any items they are unsure about to customs officials.

By understanding these entry regulations, travelers can prepare effectively and avoid complications when arriving in Lake Tahoe.

Local Currency and Exchange Rates

The local currency in the United States is the U.S. dollar (USD). For international travelers, being aware of current exchange rates is essential for budgeting and making purchases.

1. Currency Exchange: Travelers can exchange their currency at banks, currency exchange offices, or airports. However, it is important to note that airports may offer less favorable rates. To secure a better exchange rate, visitors can consider exchanging a small amount of cash before arrival and then finding a local bank or exchange service once in Lake Tahoe.

2. Credit and Debit Cards: Most businesses in Lake Tahoe accept major credit and debit cards, making it convenient for travelers to pay for meals, accommodations, and activities without needing to carry large amounts of cash. However, travelers should inform their banks of their travel plans to avoid any issues with card usage abroad.

3. ATMs: ATMs are widely available throughout Lake Tahoe. Travelers can withdraw cash as needed, but they should be aware of any foreign transaction fees that their banks may impose.

By understanding currency exchange options and using cards wisely, travelers can manage their finances effectively while enjoying their time in Lake Tahoe.

Language Tips and Communication

While English is the primary language spoken in the United States, travelers may encounter various dialects and accents. Here are some tips for effective communication:

1. Basic English Phrases: Knowing a few basic phrases in English can help non-English speakers navigate their surroundings. Simple greetings, questions, and phrases such as "thank you" and "excuse me" can enhance interactions with locals.

2. Translation Apps: For travelers who are not fluent in English, using translation apps can be very helpful. Apps like Google Translate can assist with translating signs, menus, and conversations, making it easier to communicate effectively.

3. Local Etiquette: Understanding local customs and etiquette can improve communication. For example, maintaining eye contact during conversations is considered polite in American culture, and it is customary to greet others with a friendly smile.

By being prepared with language tips, travelers can feel more confident in their interactions and enhance their overall experience in Lake Tahoe.

Suggested Budget and Money-Saving Advice

Travelers should establish a budget before visiting Lake Tahoe to ensure they can enjoy their trip without overspending. Here are some factors to consider:

1. Accommodation Costs: Prices for accommodations can vary significantly depending on the season. Budget options like motels and hostels are available, as well as upscale hotels and vacation rentals. Travelers should research and book their stays in advance to secure the best rates.

2. Dining Expenses: Dining costs can also vary. Travelers can choose from various options, ranging from fast food to fine dining. Exploring local diners and food trucks can provide delicious meals at lower prices.

3. Activities and Attractions: Many outdoor activities in Lake Tahoe are free or low-cost, such as hiking, swimming, and beach outings. For paid attractions, purchasing a day pass or looking for package deals can lead to savings.

4. Transportation: Renting a car may be necessary for those wanting to explore more remote areas of Lake Tahoe. However, travelers should also consider using public transport or ride-sharing services to save on transportation costs.

By planning a budget and being mindful of spending, travelers can enjoy their time in Lake Tahoe without financial stress.

Tips on Packing and What to Bring

Packing appropriately for a trip to Lake Tahoe is essential for a comfortable and enjoyable experience. Here are some tips on what to include:

1. Clothing: The weather in Lake Tahoe can vary significantly, so packing layers is key. Visitors should include lightweight clothing for warm days, along with warmer clothing and a waterproof jacket for cooler evenings and potential rain.

2. Outdoor Gear: For those planning outdoor activities, packing appropriate gear is vital. This includes sturdy hiking boots, swimwear, sunscreen, and a reusable water bottle. Travelers engaging in winter sports should also pack skis or snowboards, along with proper winter clothing.

3. Personal Items: Toiletries, medications, and any personal items should be included in the packing list. Additionally, travelers should remember to bring chargers for electronic devices and any necessary travel documents.

4. Snacks and Drinks: Having snacks and drinks on hand can be beneficial during travel and outdoor excursions. Packing non-perishable snacks can help save money and provide energy during long hikes or day trips.

By preparing a comprehensive packing list, travelers can ensure they have everything they need for a successful visit to Lake Tahoe.

In conclusion, understanding entry and visa requirements, local currency, language tips, budgeting, and packing essentials are fundamental for a successful trip to Lake Tahoe. By being informed and prepared, travelers can enjoy their time in this stunning destination without unnecessary stress. With the right knowledge, Lake Tahoe can be a place of adventure, relaxation, and unforgettable memories.

Chapter Twenty

Google Maps and Navigational Tools

Navigating a new destination can sometimes be overwhelming, especially in a picturesque area like Lake Tahoe, where stunning landscapes and various activities await. This chapter focuses on using Google Maps and other navigational tools to help travelers find their way around Lake Tahoe effectively. With its vast natural beauty and numerous attractions, having the right navigation tools can make a significant difference in a traveler's experience.

Google Maps provides detailed directions, real-time traffic updates, and insights into popular locations. For those venturing into remote areas or planning outdoor activities, knowing how to use maps offline can enhance the overall trip. Custom maps can also assist in finding hiking and cycling trails, ensuring that travelers can make the most of their time in Lake Tahoe.

Understanding how to navigate efficiently can turn a potentially stressful situation into an enjoyable adventure. This chapter will guide travelers through the best practices for using Google Maps and other navigational tools in Lake Tahoe.

Using Google Maps to Navigate Lake Tahoe

Google Maps is an essential tool for travelers in Lake Tahoe. It provides detailed maps, directions, and helpful information about the area. Here are some key features that can help:

1. Real-Time Directions: Google Maps offers real-time navigation, helping travelers reach their destinations with ease. Users can input their starting point and destination to receive turn-by-turn directions, whether driving, walking, or biking. The app also provides estimated travel times, which can help travelers plan their schedules.

2. Traffic Updates: Traffic conditions can vary, especially during peak tourist seasons. Google Maps provides live traffic information, allowing users to see if there are any delays on their routes. This feature enables travelers to choose alternate paths, reducing wait times and frustration.

3. Public Transportation: For those who prefer not to drive, Google Maps can help navigate public transportation options. It provides information about local bus routes, schedules, and stops, making it easier for travelers to explore the area without a car.

By utilizing Google Maps, travelers can navigate Lake Tahoe confidently, ensuring they do not miss any attractions or scenic routes along the way.

Key Locations and Points of Interest

Lake Tahoe is home to a variety of landmarks, recreational areas, and hidden gems. Google Maps can help travelers find these key locations and points of interest, enhancing their experience. Some must-see attractions include:

1. Lake Tahoe Beaches: The lake is surrounded by beautiful beaches, including Kings Beach, Sand Harbor, and Emerald Bay. Google Maps can provide directions to these popular spots, where visitors can relax, swim, or enjoy water sports.

2. Scenic Overlooks: There are numerous scenic overlooks around Lake Tahoe, such as Cave Rock and Emerald Bay State Park. These locations offer breathtaking views and are perfect for taking photographs. Google Maps can help travelers navigate to these overlooks easily.

3. Hiking Trails: Lake Tahoe has an abundance of hiking trails catering to different skill levels. Popular trails like the Tahoe Rim Trail and Eagle Lake Trail can be found on Google Maps, allowing travelers to plan their hikes accordingly.

4. Dining and Shopping: Travelers can discover local restaurants, cafes, and shops in towns like South Lake Tahoe, Stateline, and Tahoe City. Google Maps can provide reviews, hours of operation, and directions, making it easier to find dining options and shopping experiences.

Using Google Maps to pinpoint these key locations ensures that travelers can maximize their time in Lake Tahoe, visiting all the highlights that make this destination special.

Offline Maps and Tips for Remote Areas

While internet connectivity is generally reliable in Lake Tahoe, there may be areas with limited access, especially in more remote locations. Here are some tips for using offline maps effectively:

1. Download Maps in Advance: Before heading to areas with weak signals, travelers should download Google Maps for offline use. This allows them to access map data without needing an internet connection. Users can do this by selecting the desired area on Google Maps, tapping the menu, and choosing "Offline maps."

2. Familiarize with Key Routes: Knowing the main routes and destinations before going offline can help travelers feel more confident navigating. They can mark important locations, such as lodging, attractions, and rest stops, to make it easier to find them later.

3. Offline Trail Maps: For those planning outdoor activities like hiking or biking, downloading trail maps from other apps or websites in advance is beneficial. Apps such as AllTrails or Komoot provide detailed trail information, which can be accessed offline.

By preparing for offline navigation, travelers can ensure they remain oriented and informed, even in areas with limited connectivity.

Custom Maps for Hiking and Cycling Trails

Travelers looking to experience Lake Tahoe's outdoor beauty can benefit from custom maps tailored to hiking and cycling trails. Here are some tips for creating and using these maps:

1. Using Google My Maps: Travelers can create custom maps using Google My Maps. This tool allows users to mark specific trails, viewpoints, and other points of interest. They can add notes or descriptions for each location, making it easier to remember details during their adventure.

2. Trail-Specific Apps: Many apps provide specific trail maps for hiking and cycling in Lake Tahoe. These apps often include features such as elevation profiles, user reviews, and safety information. Popular options include AllTrails and Trailforks, which can help travelers choose the best routes for their skill levels.

3. Local Visitor Centers: Visitor centers in Lake Tahoe often provide printed maps of trails and cycling routes. These maps can serve as a useful backup for those who prefer physical copies. Additionally, staff can offer recommendations based on current trail conditions.

Custom maps tailored to individual interests can enhance outdoor experiences, ensuring that travelers can navigate trails safely and efficiently.

Tips for Navigating Island Areas

Lake Tahoe has several islands and unique locations that travelers may want to visit. Navigating these areas may require a different approach, and Google Maps can assist in this regard. Here are some tips:

1. Ferry Services: For those wanting to visit islands like Emerald Bay, knowing about ferry services is essential. Google Maps can help locate ferry terminals and provide schedules for those planning to take boat trips.

2. Local Guides: Some island areas may be less accessible or require specific knowledge to navigate. Travelers should consider hiring local guides or participating in guided tours. Guides often know the area well and can enhance the experience by sharing insights and ensuring safety.

3. Water Navigation: For travelers who wish to kayak or paddleboard to island areas, using maps that detail water routes can be helpful. Google Maps can assist in finding rental services for watercraft and provide directions to launch sites.

By following these tips, travelers can confidently navigate island areas, ensuring they do not miss out on the unique experiences Lake Tahoe has to offer.

In conclusion, utilizing Google Maps and other navigational tools can greatly enhance a traveler's experience in Lake Tahoe. From real-time directions to offline capabilities, these tools provide essential support in exploring the area. By understanding key locations, preparing for remote areas, creating custom maps, and navigating island areas, travelers can ensure a smooth and enjoyable visit. With the right navigational strategies in place, Lake Tahoe can become a memorable destination filled with adventure and discovery.

Chapter Twenty-One

Adventure Sports

Lake Tahoe is a premier destination for adventure sports, attracting thrill-seekers and outdoor enthusiasts from all over the world. The area offers a diverse range of activities that cater to various interests and skill levels, from high-energy pursuits to more leisurely explorations. This chapter highlights the exciting adventure sports available in and around Lake Tahoe, emphasizing the unique experiences they provide.

Adventure sports in this beautiful region allow visitors to immerse themselves in the stunning natural landscape while participating in exhilarating activities. Whether it is scaling rock faces, gliding through the air, or navigating waterways, Lake Tahoe provides countless opportunities for both seasoned athletes and newcomers to try something new. Engaging in these activities not only promotes physical fitness but also encourages appreciation for the breathtaking surroundings.

Travelers looking to make the most of their time in Lake Tahoe can benefit from the variety of adventure sports available. This chapter will delve into specific activities, explaining their appeal and offering practical information for those eager to join in on the action.

Rock Climbing and Mountaineering

Rock climbing and mountaineering are popular activities in Lake Tahoe, appealing to both novices and experienced climbers. The region is home to several climbing spots, offering various routes that suit different skill levels. Some key highlights include:

1. Diverse Climbing Routes: Lake Tahoe boasts numerous climbing locations, such as Donner Summit and the Eagle Lake Trail. These sites feature a range of climbing options, from beginner-friendly bouldering to challenging multi-pitch climbs. Climbers can find everything from granite walls to mixed terrain, providing a thrilling experience for every level.

2. Guided Climbing Experiences: For those new to climbing or looking to improve their skills, guided climbing tours are available. Experienced guides provide instruction, equipment, and safety training, ensuring that climbers feel secure and supported. These tours often take participants to less crowded areas, enhancing the overall experience.

3. Mountaineering Opportunities: In addition to rock climbing, Lake Tahoe offers mountaineering adventures for those seeking to summit local peaks. Popular routes include Mount Tallac and Mount Rose, which provide stunning views of the surrounding landscape. Hikers looking for a challenge can tackle these routes during the warmer months, while winter ascents require specialized gear and skills.

4. Safety Precautions: Climbers need to prioritize safety while enjoying these activities. Wearing proper gear, understanding climbing techniques, and being aware of weather conditions are crucial for a successful outing. For beginners, joining a climbing class can provide a solid foundation for safe climbing practices.

By engaging in rock climbing and mountaineering, travelers can experience the thrill of conquering natural obstacles while taking in the breathtaking views of Lake Tahoe.

Paragliding and Skydiving

For those who seek a truly unforgettable experience, paragliding and skydiving offer breathtaking perspectives of Lake Tahoe from above. These aerial activities allow participants to soar over the stunning landscape, providing an exhilarating rush of adrenaline.

1. Paragliding Adventures: Paragliding in Lake Tahoe provides a unique opportunity to glide through the air while taking in panoramic views of the lake and surrounding mountains. Several companies offer tandem flights, where an experienced pilot guides participants through the experience. This activity is suitable for individuals with no prior experience, as safety measures are always a priority.

2. Skydiving Experiences: Skydiving over Lake Tahoe is an extraordinary adventure that offers an adrenaline rush like no other. Participants can jump from a plane at high altitudes, experiencing freefall before parachuting down to the ground. Many skydiving companies provide tandem jumps for beginners, allowing them to jump alongside a certified instructor.

3. Scenic Views: Both paragliding and skydiving provide incredible views of Lake Tahoe's crystal-clear waters, lush forests, and surrounding mountains. The combination of breathtaking scenery and the thrill of being airborne creates a memorable experience for participants.

4. Safety Considerations: Safety is paramount in both paragliding and skydiving. All participants must undergo a safety briefing before their adventure, ensuring they understand the procedures and equipment. Reputable companies adhere to strict safety standards, providing peace of mind for participants.

Paragliding and skydiving allow travelers to experience Lake Tahoe from a new perspective, making for an exhilarating addition to any adventure sports itinerary.

Cross-Country Skiing and Snowshoeing

During the winter months, Lake Tahoe transforms into a winter wonderland, offering fantastic opportunities for cross-country skiing and snowshoeing. These activities provide a unique way to enjoy the serene beauty of the snow-covered landscape.

1. Cross-Country Skiing Trails: Lake Tahoe features an extensive network of cross-country skiing trails that cater to all skill levels. Popular spots, such as the Tahoe Cross Country Ski Area, offer groomed trails and rentals, making it easy for visitors to get started. Cross-country skiing provides an excellent cardiovascular workout while allowing participants to take in the stunning surroundings.

2. Snowshoeing Adventures: For those who prefer a slower pace, snowshoeing is an accessible and enjoyable way to experience the winter scenery. Many trails throughout the area are designated for snowshoeing, and rental equipment is widely available. Snowshoeing allows travelers to traverse snowy landscapes and enjoy the peacefulness of nature.

3. Guided Tours: For those looking to enhance their experience, guided cross-country skiing and snowshoeing tours are available. Knowledgeable guides can lead participants to hidden gems and share insights about the local flora and fauna. These tours can cater to various skill levels, making them suitable for families and beginners.

4. Winter Safety Tips: As with any outdoor activity, safety is important in cross-country skiing and snowshoeing. Participants should dress in layers, wear appropriate footwear, and stay hydrated. It is also advisable to familiarize oneself with the trails and check weather conditions before heading out.

Cross-country skiing and snowshoeing in Lake Tahoe provide a fantastic way to enjoy the beauty of winter while staying active and healthy.

Kayaking and Paddleboarding

When the warmer months arrive, Lake Tahoe's pristine waters invite travelers to partake in kayaking and paddleboarding. These activities allow individuals to connect with nature while enjoying the lake's stunning scenery.

1. Kayaking Adventures: Kayaking on Lake Tahoe offers a unique way to explore the lake's crystal-clear waters. Visitors can rent kayaks from various locations around the lake and choose from guided tours or independent paddling experiences. Paddling along the shoreline allows participants to discover secluded coves and beaches that are often inaccessible by land.

2. Paddleboarding Experiences: Stand-up paddleboarding (SUP) is another popular activity on Lake Tahoe. This relaxing and enjoyable sport is suitable for all skill levels. Rentals and lessons are widely available, making it easy for beginners to get started. Paddleboarding provides a great workout while allowing participants to take in the breathtaking views of the surrounding mountains.

3. Scenic Routes: Several scenic routes are ideal for kayaking and paddleboarding, including the shores of Sand Harbor and Emerald Bay. These locations offer stunning views and opportunities to spot wildlife, such as birds and fish. Exploring these areas by kayak or paddleboard can create a memorable experience for all participants.

4. Safety Considerations: Safety should always be a priority when kayaking and paddleboarding. Participants should wear life jackets, especially in deeper waters, and be aware of weather conditions. Staying hydrated and protecting against sun exposure is also important for a safe and enjoyable outing.
Kayaking and paddleboarding in Lake Tahoe allow travelers to immerse themselves in the natural beauty of the region while enjoying a fun and active experience on the water.

Off-Road and ATV Adventures

For those seeking an adrenaline rush on land, off-road adventures and ATV (All-Terrain Vehicle) riding provide excitement in the rugged landscapes surrounding Lake Tahoe. These activities allow participants to explore the beauty of the region while enjoying the thrill of driving through challenging terrain.

1. ATV Rentals and Tours: Several companies offer ATV rentals and guided tours in the Lake Tahoe area. These tours often lead participants through stunning backcountry trails, providing access to areas that may be difficult to reach by foot or standard vehicles. Knowledgeable guides enhance the experience by sharing insights about the region's history and wildlife.

2. Diverse Terrain: The terrain around Lake Tahoe varies from sandy trails to rocky paths, making it suitable for ATV enthusiasts of all skill levels. Riders can experience the thrill of navigating through forests, hills, and open areas, all while enjoying the stunning views of the surrounding mountains and lake.

3. Safety Gear and Practices: Safety is essential when participating in off-road adventures. Wearing appropriate safety gear, including helmets and protective clothing, is crucial for minimizing the risk of injury. Following the instructions of guides and being aware of the surroundings ensures a safe and enjoyable experience.

4. Environmental Considerations: Riders should always be mindful of the environment while engaging in off-road activities. Staying on designated trails and following local regulations helps protect the natural landscape for future visitors.

Off-road and ATV adventures offer travelers an exhilarating way to experience the rugged beauty of Lake Tahoe, making it a must-try activity for adrenaline seekers.

In conclusion, adventure sports in Lake Tahoe provide a range of thrilling experiences for all types of travelers. From rock climbing and paragliding to winter sports and water activities, there is something for everyone to enjoy. Participating in these activities allows individuals to immerse themselves in the stunning natural landscape while staying active and engaged. With so many options available, travelers are encouraged to seize the opportunity to try something new and make lasting memories in this beautiful region. Whether it's scaling a mountain, gliding through the air, or navigating serene waters, Lake Tahoe promises an unforgettable adventure for all.

Chapter Twenty-Two

Wildlife and Nature

Lake Tahoe is renowned not only for its breathtaking beauty but also for its rich and diverse wildlife. The region's unique ecosystems provide a habitat for a variety of animals, from majestic mammals to colorful birds. In this chapter, readers will discover the local wildlife that can be spotted around the lake, along with opportunities for birdwatching, visits to nature reserves, and participation in eco-tours. The beauty of Lake Tahoe's natural environment invites individuals to appreciate and understand the intricate relationships between wildlife and their habitats.

Understanding the importance of conservation is essential for protecting the area's wildlife. Many organizations work tirelessly to preserve the natural beauty and biodiversity of Lake Tahoe. This chapter will shed light on these efforts, as well as provide practical tips for wildlife photography, allowing visitors to capture their memories of this stunning location.

Engaging with Lake Tahoe's wildlife and natural environment offers an enriching experience. Whether it's observing animals in their habitats, participating in eco-tours, or capturing stunning photographs, there are numerous ways to connect with nature in this remarkable area.

Local Wildlife You Can Spot Around the Lake

Lake Tahoe is home to a variety of wildlife, making it an exciting destination for nature lovers. Visitors may encounter a range of animals during their time at the lake, including:

1. Mammals: The area boasts an array of mammals, such as black bears, mule deer, coyotes, and raccoons. Black bears are particularly iconic, and while they are often shy, spotting one can be a thrilling experience. Deer are frequently seen grazing in the meadows, especially in the early morning or late afternoon when they are most active.

2. Aquatic Animals: The clear waters of Lake Tahoe support various fish species, including Lahontan cutthroat trout, mackinaw, and rainbow trout. Fishing is a popular activity, and many anglers come to the lake in search of these native fish. The lake's ecosystems also support other aquatic life, including frogs and various invertebrates.

3. Reptiles and Amphibians: The diverse habitats around the lake are home to several reptile and amphibian species. Visitors may spot snakes, lizards, and different types of frogs. These creatures often play essential roles in the local ecosystems, contributing to the balance of nature.

4. Observation Tips: To enhance wildlife spotting, visitors should remain quiet and patient. Early morning and late afternoon are typically the best times for observing animals, as many are most active during these hours. Using binoculars or a zoom lens can help provide a better view without disturbing the wildlife.

Lake Tahoe's rich variety of wildlife provides endless opportunities for visitors to connect with nature and gain a deeper appreciation for the environment.

Birdwatching Opportunities

Lake Tahoe offers excellent birdwatching opportunities for enthusiasts of all levels. The diverse habitats around the lake attract numerous bird species, making it a fantastic location for observing these beautiful creatures.

1. Common Bird Species: Birdwatchers may encounter a range of species, including ospreys, bald eagles, American kestrels, and various songbirds. The lake's shoreline and surrounding forests provide ideal habitats for both migratory and resident birds.

2. Best Birdwatching Locations: Some of the best spots for birdwatching include the Tahoe National Forest, Emerald Bay State Park, and the shores of Sand Harbor. These areas provide diverse environments where different bird species can be observed.

3. Seasonal Considerations: Different bird species can be seen throughout the year, with migration seasons providing particularly exciting opportunities. Spring and fall are prime times for birdwatching, as many species pass through the area during these months. Keeping an eye on local birdwatching reports can help enthusiasts know what to look for during their visit.

4. Birdwatching Etiquette: To ensure a positive experience for both the birds and other observers, it is essential to follow birdwatching etiquette. Staying quiet, keeping a respectful distance from nests and feeding areas, and minimizing disturbances are crucial for protecting local wildlife.

Birdwatching in Lake Tahoe offers a peaceful way to connect with nature while appreciating the diverse avian life that calls the area home.

Nature Reserves and Protected Areas

Nature reserves and protected areas around Lake Tahoe play a vital role in preserving the region's ecosystems and wildlife habitats. These areas provide sanctuary for both plants and animals, helping to maintain the area's natural beauty.

1. Tahoe National Forest: Spanning over 800,000 acres, Tahoe National Forest offers a variety of ecosystems, including meadows, forests, and alpine environments. The forest provides numerous trails for hiking and exploring, allowing visitors to immerse themselves in nature while observing local wildlife.

2. Emerald Bay State Park: This stunning park is a designated natural reserve that protects the unique ecosystems around Emerald Bay. Visitors can hike the trails, enjoy breathtaking views, and learn about the area's flora and fauna through informational displays.

3. Conservation Efforts: Several organizations work to protect Lake Tahoe's natural resources and promote conservation. Programs focus on preserving habitats, restoring native species, and educating the public about the importance of protecting the environment.

4. Visitor Guidelines: When visiting nature reserves, it is essential to follow guidelines to protect the habitats and wildlife. Staying on designated trails, packing out trash, and respecting wildlife by observing from a distance are important practices for preserving these natural spaces.

Nature reserves and protected areas provide valuable opportunities for visitors to experience the beauty of Lake Tahoe while contributing to the preservation of its unique ecosystems.

Guided Eco-Tours and Conservation Efforts

Guided eco-tours offer visitors a chance to learn about the local environment and wildlife while supporting conservation efforts in the region. These tours provide educational experiences that enhance understanding of the ecosystems in and around Lake Tahoe.

1. Types of Eco-Tours: Various guided tours are available, including nature walks, wildlife-watching excursions, and educational boat tours on the lake. Knowledgeable guides share insights about the area's history, ecology, and wildlife, creating a deeper appreciation for the environment.

2. Conservation Initiatives: Many eco-tour companies partner with local organizations to promote conservation and sustainability. Tour participants often contribute to these efforts through fees that support habitat restoration, wildlife monitoring, and educational programs.

3. Benefits of Participation: Joining a guided eco-tour provides a unique way to connect with nature while supporting conservation initiatives. Participants gain valuable knowledge about the local ecosystem, which can inspire them to take action in their communities.

4. Family-Friendly Options: Eco-tours are suitable for all ages, making them a great family activity. Many companies offer programs tailored to children, encouraging curiosity and environmental stewardship from a young age.

Participating in guided eco-tours allows visitors to enrich their experience in Lake Tahoe while contributing to the ongoing efforts to protect the area's natural beauty.

Wildlife Photography Tips

Capturing the beauty of Lake Tahoe's wildlife through photography can be a rewarding experience. With the right techniques and knowledge, visitors can take stunning photographs that showcase the region's natural splendor.

1. Camera Equipment: A good camera and lens are essential for wildlife photography. A telephoto lens allows photographers to capture images from a distance, reducing the chance of disturbing the animals. Additionally, a tripod can provide stability, especially when shooting in low-light conditions.

2. Understanding Animal Behavior: To photograph wildlife successfully, it is crucial to understand animal behavior. Knowing when animals are most active and familiarizing oneself with their habitats can help photographers anticipate good photo opportunities.

3. Patience and Timing: Wildlife photography often requires patience. Waiting quietly for the right moment can lead to spectacular shots. Early morning or late afternoon light provides softer, more flattering lighting for photographs, enhancing the overall quality of the images.

4. Respecting Wildlife: Ethical wildlife photography involves respecting the animals and their habitats. Keeping a safe distance, avoiding loud noises, and not interfering with natural behaviors are essential practices for responsible photography.

By following these tips, visitors can capture the beauty of Lake Tahoe's wildlife while creating lasting memories of their experiences in this incredible natural environment.

In summary, Lake Tahoe's wildlife and natural surroundings offer endless opportunities for adventure and appreciation. From spotting local wildlife and enjoying birdwatching to visiting nature reserves and participating in eco-tours, there are many ways to connect with the environment. The region's conservation efforts ensure that future generations can continue to experience the beauty and diversity of Lake Tahoe. For anyone visiting, taking the time to engage with the local wildlife and nature is highly recommended. Whether through photography, guided tours, or simply observing the wildlife, there is much to discover and appreciate in this remarkable area.

Chapter Twenty-Three

Camping and RV Trips

Camping and RV trips around Lake Tahoe offer an excellent way to experience the natural beauty and outdoor adventures this area has to offer. Lake Tahoe is surrounded by stunning landscapes, pristine waters, and majestic mountains, making it a prime destination for those looking to immerse themselves in nature. This chapter aims to provide valuable insights into the best camping spots and RV-friendly locations, ensuring a memorable outdoor experience for families and adventurers alike.

Best Camping Spots Around the Lake

Lake Tahoe is home to numerous camping spots, each providing unique experiences. From the shores of the lake to the heights of the mountains, there is a place for everyone.

1. D.L. Bliss State Park: This campground is known for its breathtaking views and access to beautiful beaches. The park features sites nestled among towering trees, offering a perfect blend of privacy and nature. Visitors can enjoy swimming, hiking, and exploring the nearby trails.

2. Emerald Bay State Park: Famous for its stunning bay and the iconic Vikingsholm Castle, this park provides a picturesque camping experience. Campers can hike to viewpoints overlooking the bay and visit Fannette Island. The combination of history and natural beauty makes this spot a favorite among many.

3. Sugar Pine Point State Park: This site offers a more secluded camping experience. The campground is located near the lake and features a mix of tent and RV sites. There are also several trails for hiking and biking, perfect for those wanting to experience the surrounding wilderness.

4. Lake Tahoe Basin Management Unit: This area offers multiple campgrounds managed by the US Forest Service. Sites here are often less crowded and provide a genuine camping experience. Campers can enjoy hiking, fishing, and wildlife watching, all within proximity to the lake.

5. Tahoe National Forest: Located to the northwest of Lake Tahoe, this forest provides a variety of campgrounds suitable for tent camping and

RVs. The forest is vast, offering numerous trails and opportunities for outdoor activities, including mountain biking and fishing.

RV-Friendly Locations and Facilities

For those traveling in RVs, Lake Tahoe offers several RV-friendly locations that cater to the needs of these travelers. Here are some notable spots:

1. Campground by the Lake: Located in South Lake Tahoe, this RV park provides full hookups and amenities like showers and laundry facilities. It is close to the lake, making it a convenient base for activities.

2. Tahoe Valley Campground: This family-friendly campground features spaces for RVs, tent camping, and various facilities. There are amenities such as a swimming pool, playgrounds, and recreational areas for families to enjoy.

3. Zephyr Cove Resort: Situated on the east shore of Lake Tahoe, this resort offers RV sites with stunning lake views. Visitors can also enjoy water sports, beach access, and dining options nearby.

4. Meeks Bay Resort: This location provides RV spots with beautiful views of the lake. The resort has amenities like restrooms, showers, and a small store. It is also an excellent place for outdoor activities such as hiking and swimming.

5. Lake Tahoe KOA: Known for its exceptional amenities, this KOA location features spacious RV sites, cabins, and tent camping. Guests can enjoy swimming pools, bike rentals, and organized activities for children.

Tips for Camping with Kids

Camping with children can be an exciting adventure, but it also requires planning to ensure everyone has a good time. Here are some tips to help families have a smooth camping experience:

1. Involve Kids in Planning: Allowing children to help plan the trip can increase their excitement. Let them choose activities and sites they want to visit, fostering a sense of ownership in the adventure.

2. Pack Smart: Bring essentials like comfortable sleeping gear, games, and outdoor toys. A first aid kit is also important. Consider including kid-friendly snacks to keep them energized during hikes and activities.

3. Keep Activities Engaging: Plan a mix of activities to keep kids entertained. Nature scavenger hunts, storytelling around the campfire, and short hikes can provide fun and educational experiences.

4. Safety First: Teach children about safety in the wilderness. Discuss the importance of staying close to the campsite, recognizing wildlife, and respecting nature.

5. Flexible Schedule: While having a plan is essential, being flexible can lead to unexpected fun. Children might enjoy spontaneous activities, so be open to changes.

Campfire Safety and Regulations

Campfires are a cherished part of the camping experience, but safety and regulations are critical to ensure a safe environment for all campers. Here are important points to consider:

1. Follow Local Regulations: Before starting a campfire, check the regulations specific to the campground. Some areas may have fire restrictions due to dry conditions.

2. Select a Safe Location: Use designated fire pits when available. If a pit is not provided, create a safe area away from tents and overhanging branches.

3. Keep it Small: A small fire is easier to control and reduces the risk of wildfires. Use only the wood provided by the campground or gathered within regulations.

4. Supervise Children: Always keep a close eye on children around the fire. Teach them the importance of fire safety and ensure they stay at a safe distance.

5. Extinguish Properly: When finished, ensure the fire is completely out. Douse it with water and stir the ashes to make sure no embers remain.

Top Hikes Near Campgrounds

Lake Tahoe is renowned for its hiking trails, offering paths suitable for all skill levels. Here are some of the best hikes near popular campgrounds:

1. Eagle Lake Trail: This short hike is ideal for families. It leads to a stunning alpine lake and is a great introduction to hiking for kids. The trailhead is near Eagle Lake Campground, making it a convenient option.

2. Mount Tallac Trail: For those seeking a more challenging hike, the Mount Tallac Trail offers incredible views of Lake Tahoe from the summit. While this hike is more strenuous, it rewards adventurers with breathtaking panoramas.

3. Rubicon Trail: Starting near D.L. Bliss State Park, this trail provides stunning views of the lake and is accessible for families. The hike offers opportunities for swimming along the way, making it a great summer adventure.

4. Emerald Bay Trail: This scenic trail leads to viewpoints of Emerald Bay and Vikingsholm Castle. It is a moderately challenging hike, perfect for those looking to combine exercise with sightseeing.

5. Tahoe Rim Trail: A section of this extensive trail runs near several campgrounds, offering both short and long hiking options. The trail provides beautiful vistas and a chance to encounter local wildlife.

Camping and RV trips around Lake Tahoe present a wonderful opportunity to connect with nature and create lasting memories. With careful planning and awareness of safety guidelines, families and adventurers can enjoy all that this remarkable region has to offer. The stunning scenery, diverse activities, and welcoming campgrounds make it an ideal destination for outdoor enthusiasts of all ages.

Chapter Twenty-Four

Lake Tahoe Nightlife

Lake Tahoe is not only famous for its stunning natural beauty and outdoor activities but also for its vibrant nightlife. As the sun sets behind the mountains and the stars light up the sky, the region transforms into a lively hub of entertainment. Whether it is a cozy evening with friends at a lakefront bar, a thrilling night of gaming at a casino, or enjoying live music performances, Lake Tahoe offers something for everyone after dark. This chapter will provide insights into the best nightlife options available in the area, ensuring that visitors can enjoy every moment of their stay.

Best Places for Evening Entertainment

Lake Tahoe has numerous spots that cater to different tastes when it comes to evening entertainment. Each venue provides a unique atmosphere, making it easy to find the perfect place to unwind after a day of activities.

1. Heavenly Village: This bustling area features various restaurants, shops, and entertainment options. Visitors can stroll through the village, enjoy a meal at one of the many restaurants, and then catch a live performance or movie at the nearby cinema. The vibrant atmosphere makes it a popular choice for locals and tourists alike.

2. Stateline, Nevada: Known for its lively nightlife, Stateline is home to several bars and clubs. Visitors can dance the night away at popular nightclubs or enjoy cocktails in more relaxed settings. This area is known for its lively atmosphere, making it a favorite among those looking for a good time.

3. South Lake Tahoe: This area offers a diverse range of evening activities, from quiet bars to energetic dance clubs. Many establishments host themed nights and special events, providing a fun environment for all. Whether it's a pub with local brews or a trendy club with a DJ, there's something for everyone.

4. Tahoe City: For those seeking a more laid-back evening, Tahoe City offers charming bars and restaurants with beautiful views of the lake. Visitors can enjoy a quiet dinner followed by drinks while watching the sunset over the water.

5. North Lake Tahoe: This region is known for its intimate venues and community events. Visitors can often find local bands playing at small bars and restaurants, providing a cozy and welcoming atmosphere.

Lakefront Bars and Lounges

Enjoying a drink by the lake is a must while visiting Lake Tahoe. Several bars and lounges offer stunning views of the water and a relaxing ambiance. Here are some of the best spots to consider:

1. The Beach House: Located on the shores of the lake, this bar provides a relaxed setting with outdoor seating. Guests can enjoy cocktails and light bites while taking in the beautiful sunset. The sound of the waves adds to the soothing atmosphere.

2. Gar Woods Grill & Pier: This lakeside restaurant and bar is famous for its signature drink, the "Gar Wood's Special." Guests can sit on the deck overlooking the water, making it a perfect place for a leisurely evening.

3. Heavenly Mountain Resort's Sky Deck: This venue offers breathtaking views of the lake and the surrounding mountains. The Sky Deck provides a unique experience for guests who want to enjoy a drink in a stunning setting after a day of skiing or hiking.

4. Lakeside Beach Bar: Known for its casual vibe, this bar offers a variety of beverages and light snacks. The outdoor seating allows guests to relax and soak in the beautiful scenery, making it a great spot to unwind.

5. Riva Grill: This popular lakeside restaurant features an extensive drink menu and outdoor seating with views of the lake. The vibrant atmosphere and friendly service make it a favorite among locals and tourists.

Live Music and Performances

Live music is an integral part of Lake Tahoe's nightlife. Numerous venues host performances from local bands and artists, creating a lively environment for visitors to enjoy. Here are some notable places to catch a show:

1. The Crystal Bay Club Casino: This venue hosts a variety of live music acts throughout the year. From local bands to well-known artists, there is always something happening at the Crystal Bay Club. The intimate setting allows guests to enjoy performances up close.

2. The MontBleu Theatre: This popular venue regularly features concerts and events. It attracts both big-name acts and local talent, providing an eclectic mix of entertainment options for guests. The atmosphere is electric, making it a memorable spot for music lovers.

3. Heavenly Village's Live Music Events: Throughout the summer, Heavenly Village hosts live music events in the outdoor plaza. Visitors can enjoy free concerts while sipping drinks and enjoying the vibrant atmosphere.

4. Lake Tahoe Community College: This venue hosts various cultural events, including concerts, theater performances, and art exhibitions. It is an excellent place for visitors to experience local talent and cultural offerings.

5. Local Bars: Many bars and restaurants around Lake Tahoe feature live music on weekends. These performances often include a mix of genres, from acoustic sets to rock bands, providing something for everyone.

Casino Resorts and Gaming

Lake Tahoe is known for its world-class casinos that offer a range of gaming options and entertainment. The casino resorts provide an exciting atmosphere for those looking to try their luck. Here are some notable casinos to consider:

1. Harrah's Lake Tahoe: This well-known resort features a large casino floor with table games, slots, and poker rooms. Harrah's also hosts regular entertainment events, including live music and shows, making it a popular destination for both gaming and entertainment.

2. MontBleu Resort Casino: In addition to its gaming options, MontBleu offers a vibrant nightlife scene with bars and lounges. Visitors can enjoy drinks and dance the night away after trying their luck at the tables.

3. Stateline Casinos: Several casinos in Stateline offer a variety of gaming options, including blackjack, roulette, and poker. The lively atmosphere and numerous dining options make these casinos a great choice for an exciting night out.

4. Tahoe Nugget: This smaller casino provides a friendly and welcoming atmosphere. While it may not be the same size as larger casinos, it offers a variety of gaming options and often hosts special events.

5. Lake Tahoe Casino Tour: For those looking to experience multiple casinos in one night, guided casino tours are available. These tours often include transportation and allow guests to visit several casinos, and try different games and entertainment.

Night Cruises on the Lake

One of the most enchanting ways to experience Lake Tahoe at night is by taking a night cruise. These cruises offer stunning views of the illuminated shoreline and the starry sky above. Here are some popular options for night cruises:

1. Lake Tahoe Dinner Cruises: Several companies offer dinner cruises that include a meal and entertainment. Guests can enjoy a delicious dinner while taking in the breathtaking views of the lake and surrounding mountains.

2. Sunset Cruises: These cruises allow visitors to watch the sun dip below the horizon while enjoying drinks and music. The views during sunset are truly spectacular, making it a romantic option for couples.

3. Fireworks Cruises: During certain holidays and events, fireworks cruises offer guests the chance to enjoy a fireworks display from the water. This unique experience is perfect for those looking to celebrate special occasions.

4. Sightseeing Cruises: Many companies offer sightseeing cruises that provide insights into the lake's history and natural beauty. These cruises often include commentary from knowledgeable guides, enhancing the experience.

5. Private Charters: For a more personalized experience, private charters are available. Guests can customize their cruise, choosing the duration, route, and amenities to create their ideal night on the water.

Lake Tahoe's nightlife is as diverse as its stunning landscapes. With a wide range of evening entertainment options, visitors are sure to find something that suits their preferences. Whether it's enjoying a drink at a lakefront bar, dancing the night away, or taking a memorable cruise on the water, Lake Tahoe offers a vibrant nightlife scene that enhances any trip. As night falls over this beautiful region, the possibilities for fun and relaxation are endless.

Chapter Twenty-Five

Transportation and Airports

In this chapter, readers will gain insight into the transportation options available in Lake Tahoe, particularly concerning the airports in the area. Understanding how to navigate from the airport to the city, the various means of transportation available, and the driving routes can significantly enhance a traveler's experience. Whether visitors choose to rent a car, take a taxi, or use public transportation, this chapter provides the necessary information for seamless travel upon arrival in Lake Tahoe.

All the Airports in the City

Lake Tahoe does not have its major airport, but several nearby airports serve as gateways to the region. The primary airports that travelers can use to reach Lake Tahoe include:

1. **Reno-Tahoe International Airport (RNO)**
- Location: Approximately 60 miles from Lake Tahoe, located in Reno, Nevada.
- Services: Major airlines operate flights to and from this airport, providing a wide range of domestic and some international destinations.

2. **Sacramento International Airport (SMF)**
- Location: Approximately 100 miles from Lake Tahoe, situated in Sacramento, California.
- Services: This airport also offers numerous flights to various domestic locations, making it a viable option for travelers heading to Lake Tahoe.

3. **Lake Tahoe Airport (TVL)**
- Location: Located in South Lake Tahoe, California, this is a smaller regional airport primarily serving private flights and some commercial flights.
- Services: Limited commercial flights are available, mainly during peak seasons.

Transportation Options in the Town on Arrival at the Airport

Once travelers arrive at the airport, they have several transportation options to reach Lake Tahoe and get around town. Here's how they can navigate their arrival:

- Car Rentals: Available at all major airports (Reno-Tahoe and Sacramento). Rental companies include major brands like Hertz, Enterprise, and Avis.
- Shuttle Services: Various shuttle companies offer direct transportation to Lake Tahoe from Reno-Tahoe and Sacramento airports. This is a convenient option for those without a rental car.
- Public Transportation: Buses run between Reno and Lake Tahoe, providing a budget-friendly option for travelers.
- Taxis and Rideshare: Taxi services are available at the airports, and rideshare options like Uber and Lyft operate in the area.

Driving Routes Around the City Airport and Nearby Towns

Travelers can use the following driving routes to navigate between the airports and Lake Tahoe:

From Reno-Tahoe International Airport:
  - Take US-395 South to I-80 East.
  - Merge onto CA-89 South, which leads directly to South Lake Tahoe.

From Sacramento International Airport:
  - Take I-5 North to I-80 East.
  - Merge onto CA-89 South to reach South Lake Tahoe.

Transportation Means at the Airport

Travelers can utilize various transportation methods upon arrival at the airports:

Car Rentals
  - Price: Varies by company, typically ranging from $30 to $100 per day, depending on the vehicle type and rental duration.
  - Location: Rental car counters are located within the airport terminals.

Taxis
   - Price: Approximately $150 to $200 from Reno to Lake Tahoe; costs may vary based on distance and traffic conditions.
   - Location: Taxi stands are located outside the airport terminals.

Shuttle Services
   - Price: Around $50 to $75 per person for one-way service to Lake Tahoe, depending on the provider.
   - Location: Shuttle pick-up areas are usually marked outside the terminal.

Public Buses
   - Price: Generally less than $30 for a one-way fare from Reno to Lake Tahoe.
   - Location: Bus stops are located outside the terminal building.

Biking
   - Price: Varies based on rental services; expect around $20 to $40 per day.
   - Location: Bike rental services may be found near popular locations or in the town.

Best Options: Hire a Car or Book a Taxi

Hire a Car:
   - Pros: Provides flexibility to explore Lake Tahoe and surrounding areas at one's own pace. Ideal for travelers planning to visit multiple attractions or nearby towns.
   - Cons: Parking fees and the need to navigate unfamiliar roads.

Book a Taxi or Shuttle:
   - Pros: Convenient for direct transportation to the hotel or destination without the need to drive. Suitable for those not planning to venture far from Lake Tahoe.
   - Cons: Less flexibility for spontaneous trips; costs can add up over multiple days.

Finally, Whereabouts (How to Go About Each Airport in the City)

Reno-Tahoe International Airport (RNO):
   - Follow signs for rental cars upon arrival.
   - Look for shuttle service signs to find transportation to Lake Tahoe.
   - Consider taking a taxi or rideshare if not renting a vehicle.

Sacramento International Airport (SMF):
- Head to the ground transportation area for shuttles and taxis.
- Rental cars are available on-site; follow the signs in the terminal.
- Public buses can be accessed at designated stops outside the terminal.

Lake Tahoe Airport (TVL):
- Local transportation options may be limited; consider arranging a shuttle or taxi in advance.
- Rental services may be available but limited compared to larger airports.

This chapter provides essential information on navigating transportation options upon arriving in Lake Tahoe, ensuring that visitors can efficiently plan their journey and enjoy their time in this beautiful destination. Whether choosing to drive, ride, or take public transit, understanding these details will enhance the overall experience and make travel easier.

Chapter Twenty-Six

Conclusion

The conclusion serves as the final chapter of this travel guide, providing readers with an opportunity to reflect on everything they have learned about Lake Tahoe. It summarizes essential travel tips and highlights the importance of experiencing the unique beauty and adventures that the area offers. This chapter aims to inspire and motivate readers to plan their journey, ensuring they take full advantage of what Lake Tahoe has to offer. With its majestic mountains, crystal-clear waters, and vibrant nightlife, Lake Tahoe stands as a destination that promises unforgettable memories for every traveler.

Summary of Key Travel Tips

Throughout the guide, several key travel tips have emerged to help visitors make the most of their time in Lake Tahoe. Understanding these tips can enhance the travel experience and ensure that visitors are well-prepared for their adventure.

1. Plan: Lake Tahoe is a popular destination, especially during peak seasons. It is advisable to book accommodations and activities in advance to secure the best options. Researching the best times to visit specific attractions can also help avoid long lines and overcrowding.

2. Dress in Layers: The weather in Lake Tahoe can change rapidly, particularly in the mountains. Dressing in layers allows travelers to adapt to varying temperatures throughout the day. This tip is especially important for outdoor activities like hiking and skiing.

3. Stay Hydrated: The high elevation of Lake Tahoe can lead to dehydration. It is essential to drink plenty of water, particularly during outdoor activities. Keeping hydrated will help maintain energy levels and enhance overall enjoyment.

4. Respect Nature: Lake Tahoe's natural beauty is one of its biggest attractions. Visitors should follow Leave No Trace principles, ensuring they do not harm the environment. This includes disposing of waste properly and respecting wildlife.

5. Be Flexible: While planning is important, being open to changes can lead to unexpected adventures. Weather conditions can impact activities, so having backup plans can help travelers enjoy their trip regardless of circumstances.

Encouragement to Enjoy and Embrace the Experience

Lake Tahoe is a place filled with opportunities for adventure, relaxation, and connection with nature. Visitors are encouraged to take full advantage of the area's offerings, whether it is hiking the scenic trails, enjoying water activities, or relaxing at a lakeside bar. Each moment spent in Lake Tahoe can become a cherished memory, making it important for travelers to engage with their surroundings and savor every experience. The beauty of the lake and the surrounding mountains creates an inspiring backdrop for relaxation and exploration.

Taking the time to appreciate the scenery, participate in local activities, and connect with fellow travelers will enrich the visit. Visitors should allow themselves the freedom to enjoy spontaneous moments, creating a personalized journey that reflects their interests and passions.

Final Thoughts and Recommendations

In conclusion, Lake Tahoe is a destination that offers something for everyone. From outdoor enthusiasts to those seeking a peaceful retreat, the region caters to a wide range of preferences. The blend of natural beauty, recreational activities, and vibrant culture makes it a unique place to visit. For travelers considering their next adventure, Lake Tahoe should be high on the list.

It is recommended to take advantage of local resources, including visitor centers and online platforms, to stay informed about events, activities, and safety guidelines. Engaging with locals can also enhance the experience, providing insights into hidden gems and must-see attractions. Ultimately, visitors should approach their journey with an open heart and a spirit of adventure.

Acknowledgments and Thanks

This guide would not be possible without the contributions of numerous individuals and organizations dedicated to preserving and promoting the beauty of Lake Tahoe. Thanks are due to local tourism boards, outdoor activity providers, and residents who have shared their knowledge and experiences, enriching this guide. Their passion for Lake Tahoe shines through in their efforts to make it a welcoming destination for travelers.

Additionally, gratitude goes to the readers for choosing this guide to assist in their journey. It is hoped that the information provided will enhance their visit and encourage them to share their experiences with others.

Contact Information for Further Assistance

For further assistance, visitors can reach out to various resources available in the Lake Tahoe area. Local tourism offices and visitor centers are excellent starting points for inquiries about accommodations, activities, and events. Here are some valuable contacts:

Lake Tahoe Visitors Authority
Website: [www.lake tahoe visitors authority.com](http://www.laketahoevisitorsauthority.com)
  Phone: 1-800-888-TRIP (8747)

Tahoe Regional Planning Agency
  Website: www.trpa.gov
  Phone: 775-588-4547

Sierra State Parks Foundation
  Website: www.sierrastateparks.org
  Phone: 530-582-1024

Local Outdoor Activity Providers:
  Many companies offer guided tours, rentals, and lessons for various outdoor activities. Checking online reviews and recommendations can lead to great experiences.

By utilizing these resources, visitors can ensure that their trip to Lake Tahoe is enjoyable, safe, and memorable. With the right preparation and an open mind, Lake Tahoe promises to be a destination filled with adventure and beauty. Whether planning a weekend getaway or an extended vacation, the opportunities for enjoyment and connection with nature are endless.

Made in the USA
Las Vegas, NV
12 December 2024

13890092R00068